# WONDERS OF
# NEW YORK

WHITE STAR PUBLISHERS

# Empty Sky: New Jersey September 11th Memorial

On the morning of September 11, 2001, with the skies so clear that the Twin Towers across the river appeared to be within reach, the very essence of what our country stands for— freedom, tolerance, and the pursuit of happiness—was attacked. This memorial is dedicated to New Jersey's innocent loved ones who were violently and senselessly murdered that day at the World Trade Center, The Pentagon, and in Shanksville, PA.

James Burns  John Paul Bocchi  Matthew T. McDermott
Alan Zampieri  Siucheung Steve Wong  Thomas Edward
Nolan  William R. Tieste  John P. Skala  Frankie Serrano
J. Binnery  Hideya Kawauchi  Joseph O. Pick  Jemal
ederer  Lloyd Rosenberg  Albert Elmarry  Scott W. Cahill
D. Diehl  Jean Peterson  Donald Peterson  Ming-Hao Liu
Gavin Fraser Cushny  Frank Joseph Doyle  Joseph John

Rosenbaum   Jennifer Louise Fialko   Chih Min "Dennis" Foo   Manuel L. Lopez

n   Kenneth Ledee   Jean Andrucki   Brian F. Hennessey   Nicholas P. Pietrunti

J. Gallagher   Michael Waye   Joseph Mangano   William F. Fallon   Masaru Ose

e De Santis   Michael Patrick LaForte   Louis F. Aversano, Jr.   Richard Rodriguez

ael Sorresse   George J. Strauch   John Schroeder   Michael Egan   Lesley Thomas

Andrew Silverstein   Alfred J. Braca   Catherine T. Smith   Sankara S. Velamur

Vincent Boland Jr.   Steven F. Schlag   Charles A. Murphy   Daniel D. Bergstein

**text by**
ALESSANDRA MATTANZA

**edited by**
VALERIA MANFERTO DE FABIANIS

**graphic layout**
MARIA CUCCHI

**editorial coordination**
LAURA ACCOMAZZO
VALENTINA GIAMMARINARO

*2-3* • Central Park is the green lung of the city right in the heart of New York.

*4-5* • On a wall of the New Jersey Empty Sky Memorial in Liberty State Park in Jersey City, there are the names of 746 inhabitants of New Jersey who died in the terrorist attack on the Twin Towers in 2001.

*9* • The Statue of Liberty has always been the symbol of New York's democratic spirit.

*10-11* • The buildings and skyscrapers of Lower Manhattan's Financial District are reflected in the waters of the river.

*12-13* • Christmas Angels that are lit up every year at Christmas to decorate the Rockefeller Center.

*14-15* • These two skyscrapers face each other on 5th Avenue.

WONDERS OF

# NEW
# YORK

# CONTENTS

## WONDERS OF NEW YORK

# Introduction

Nᴇᴡ ʏᴏʀᴋ ɪꜱ ᴀ ᴠɪᴠᴀᴄɪᴏᴜꜱ, ɪɴᴛᴇɴꜱᴇ ᴀɴᴅ ᴅᴀᴢᴢʟɪɴɢ ᴄɪᴛʏ. ᴍᴜᴄʜ ʟɪᴋᴇ ᴀ ᴄʜᴀᴍᴇʟᴇᴏɴ, ɪᴛ ᴄʜᴀɴɢᴇꜱ ᴄᴏʟᴏʀ ᴀɴᴅ ɪꜱ ᴛʀᴀɴꜱ-ꜰᴏʀᴍᴇᴅ ɪɴ ᴀɴ ɪɴꜱᴛᴀɴᴛ, ᴅᴇᴘᴇɴᴅɪɴɢ ᴏɴ ᴛʜᴇ ᴍᴏᴍᴇɴᴛ ᴀɴᴅ ᴛʜᴇ ꜱɪᴛ-ᴜᴀᴛɪᴏɴ. ɪᴛꜱ ᴇʏᴇꜱ ᴀʀᴇ ᴛʜᴇ ᴡɪɴᴅᴏᴡꜱ ᴏꜰ ᴛʜᴇ ꜱᴋʏꜱᴄʀᴀᴘᴇʀꜱ ᴛʜᴀᴛ ᴏᴠᴇʀʟᴏᴏᴋ ᴛʜᴇ ᴡᴏʀʟᴅ ʙᴇʟᴏᴡ, ʟɪᴋᴇ ᴛʜᴇ ʟɪɢʜᴛꜱ ᴛʜᴀᴛ ꜱᴇᴇᴍ ᴛᴏ ꜱᴘʏ ᴏɴ ᴜꜱ ꜰʀᴏᴍ ᴛʜᴇ ꜱɪɢɴꜱ ᴀɴᴅ ʙɪʟʟʙᴏᴀʀᴅꜱ, ʟɪᴋᴇ ᴛʜᴇ ꜰᴜᴛᴜʀɪꜱᴛɪᴄ ꜱᴜʀᴠᴇɪʟʟᴀɴᴄᴇ ᴄᴀᴍᴇʀᴀꜱ ᴛʜᴀᴛ ꜰᴏʟʟᴏᴡ ᴛʜᴇ ꜰʀᴇɴᴇᴛɪᴄ ᴍᴏᴠᴇᴍᴇɴᴛ ᴏꜰ ᴘᴇᴏᴘʟᴇ ꜱᴡᴀʀᴍɪɴɢ ᴛʜʀᴏᴜɢʜ ᴛʜᴇ ꜱᴜʙᴡᴀʏ. ᴛʜᴇ ᴍᴏᴜᴛʜ ᴏꜰ ɴᴇᴡ ʏᴏʀᴋ ᴄɪᴛʏ ɪꜱ ʀᴇᴘʀᴇꜱᴇɴᴛᴇᴅ ʙʏ ᴛʜᴇ ᴇɴᴛʀᴀɴᴄᴇꜱ ᴛᴏ ɪᴛꜱ ᴍᴀɴʏ ᴍᴜꜱᴇᴜᴍꜱ, ᴡʜɪᴄʜ ᴏᴘᴇɴ ᴇᴠᴇʀʏ ᴅᴀʏ ᴛᴏ ɢʀᴇᴇᴛ ᴍɪʟʟɪᴏɴꜱ ᴏꜰ ᴛᴏᴜʀɪꜱᴛꜱ, ᴛʜᴇ ᴅᴏᴏʀᴡᴀʏꜱ ᴏꜰ ᴛʜᴇ ꜱʜᴏᴘꜱ ᴀɴᴅ ᴅᴇᴘᴀʀᴛᴍᴇɴᴛ ꜱᴛᴏʀᴇꜱ ᴅᴏᴍɪɴᴀᴛᴇᴅ ʙʏ ᴛʜᴇ ꜱʜᴏᴘᴘɪɴɢ ᴍᴀɴɪᴀ, ᴀɴᴅ ᴛʜᴇ ᴅᴏᴏʀꜱ ᴏꜰ ᴛʜᴇ ᴇɴᴛɪᴄɪɴɢ ᴀɴᴅ ɪʀʀᴇꜱɪꜱᴛɪʙʟᴇ ᴄᴀꜰᴇ́ꜱ, ʀᴇꜱᴛᴀᴜʀᴀɴᴛꜱ ᴀɴᴅ ɴɪɢʜᴛ ᴄʟᴜʙꜱ ᴛʜᴀᴛ ᴀᴛᴛʀᴀᴄᴛ ᴀɴᴅ ʙᴇᴡɪᴛᴄʜ ʏᴏᴜ ꜰᴏʀ ʜᴏᴜʀꜱ ᴏɴ ᴇɴᴅ. ᴛʜᴇ ᴇᴀʀꜱ ᴏꜰ ᴛʜᴇ ᴄɪᴛʏ ᴀʀᴇ ɪᴛꜱ ᴅᴇꜱɪʀᴇ ᴛᴏ ᴀʙꜱᴏʀʙ ɪᴅᴇᴀꜱ, ɪᴛꜱ ᴄʀᴇᴀᴛɪᴠɪ-

• Times Square teeming with traffic.

# Introduction

TY, ITS ENTHUSIASM, WHICH MAKE IT SO MAGNETIC AND TIRELESS: THE CITY THAT NEVER SLEEPS. ITS HEART BEATS TO THE RHYTHM OF ITS MORE THAN 8 MILLION INHABITANTS (17 MILLION, INCLUDING THE ADJACENT URBAN AREAS, WHILE 18 MILLION TOURISTS VISIT THE CITY EVERY YEAR), WHO TRAVERSE IT LIKE AN ARMY OF DILIGENT ANTS AND TREAT IT AS IF IT WERE A HARD-TO-PLEASE LOVER: THEY LOVE HER, THEY HATE HER, THEY DESPISE AND CRITICIZE HER, THEY ADORE AND RESPECT HER, THEY SCRUTINIZE HER SKEPTICALLY. NEW YORK CITY IS UNPREDICTABLE AND UNCONTROLLABLE, UTTERLY OVERWHELMING.

BE THAT AS IT MAY, THERE IS NOT ONLY ONE NEW YORK CITY; THERE ARE TEN, ONE THOUSAND, ONE HUNDRED THOUSAND CITIES, AND EVERY DAY A NEW ONE IS DISCOVERED, BECAUSE NEW YORK IS ALWAYS 'NEW NEW YORK', A CITY IN CONTINUOUS EVOLUTION, IN WHICH NEW NEIGHBORHOODS ARE CREATED AND NEW TRENDS ARE BORN.

# Introduction

NEW YORK CONTINUES TO BE THE LAND OF DREAMS, ATTRACTING PEOPLE FROM ALL CORNERS OF THE WORLD WHO SEEK TO BEGIN A NEW LIFE. ITS SOUL HAS ROOTS THAT GO BACK 11,500 YEARS, WHEN THIS AREA WAS A SWAMPLAND POPULATED BY PALEO-INDIANS. THE FIRST EUROPEAN TO LAND IN THIS AREA WAS GIOVANNI DA VERRAZZANO, WHO NAVIGATED FOR THE FRENCH, ARRIVING HERE WAY BACK IN 1524. HENRY HUDSON, AN ENGLISHMAN IN THE SERVICE OF THE DUTCH WEST INDIES COMPANY, REACHED THIS AREA IN 1609 VIA THE RIVER NAMED AFTER HIM, AND THE FIRST DUTCH SETTLEMENT DATES TO 1613. IN 1626, THE GOVERNOR OF THIS COLONY, PETER MINUIT, PURCHASED THE ISLAND OF MANHATTAN FROM THE INDIANS, WHO ACCEPTED FABRICS AND TRINKETS WORTH ONLY 24 DOLLARS AS PAYMENT. THE CITY WAS NAMED NEW AMSTERDAM BY THE NEW INHABITANTS, PERHAPS BECAUSE THEY WERE NOSTALGIC ABOUT THE MOTHERLAND. NEW SETTLERS, ENGLISH QUAKERS, ARRIVED IN 1657, DURING THE GOVERNORSHIP OF PETER STUYVESANT.

# Introduction

NEW YORK TOOK ON ITS PRESENT NAME IN 1664, WHEN COLONEL RICHARD NICOLLS, AT THE BEHEST OF JAMES STUART, THE DUKE OF YORK AND BROTHER OF THE KING, INVADED THE CITY AND BECAME ITS FIRST ENGLISH GOVERNOR, NAMING IT AFTER HIS PROTECTOR. THE CITY IMMEDIATELY DISPLAYED A GREAT SPIRIT OF INDEPENDENCE AND LIBERTY, AS THE COLONISTS SOON BECAME ANTAGONISTIC TO BRITISH AUTHORITY AND LATER ASSEMBLED UNDER THE BANNER OF THE COMMANDER-IN-CHIEF OF THE REVOLUTIONARY CONTINENTAL ARMY, GEORGE WASHINGTON. AMERICAN INDEPENDENCE WAS ATTAINED IN 1783, WHEN WASHINGTON MARCHED INTO TOWN AND STAYED IN THE FRAUNCES TAVERN IN LOWER MANHATTAN, WHERE THE ATMOSPHERE OF THE PAST IS MANIFESTED IN THE HOUSES BUILT IN THAT PERIOD, NOW SURROUNDED BY TALL SKYSCRAPERS.

*22-23* • The new skyline of Lower Manhattan, has a futuristic look.

*24-25* • A jogger on the circular track in Central Park.

# Introduction

TODAY NEW YORK IS FIRST OF ALL THE SYMBOL OF LIBERTY AND WE ARE REMINDED OF THIS EVERY TIME WE SEE THE STATUE OF LIBERTY FROM BATTERY PARK (NAMED AFTER A BATTERY OF ENGLISH CANNONS PLACED THERE IN THE 18TH CENTURY AT THE CASTLE CLINTON REDOUBT, WHICH CAN STILL BE VISITED). THE STATUE STANDS ON AN ISLAND IN THE BAY. IT WAS A GIFT THE FRENCH GOVERNMENT MADE TO THE AMERICAN PEOPLE IN 1883 AND WAS INAUGURATED IN 1886. THE STATUE HOLDS A TABLET REPRESENTING THE DECLARATION OF INDEPENDENCE AND A TORCH SYMBOLIZING THE LIGHT OF REASON, WHILE THE SEVEN POINTS OF THE CROWN REPRESENT THE SEVEN CONTINENTS. 'LADY LIBERTY', THE NICKNAME FOR THIS MONUMENT, WAS THE FIRST THING IMMIGRANTS SAW UPON THEIR ARRIVAL IN THE BAY, BEFORE LANDING AT ELLIS ISLAND AND TO THIS DAY SHE REPRESENTS THE MYTH OF THE AMERICAN DREAM.

*26-27* • A view from above East River and Midtown East.

# VISIONS
## of NEW YORK

- A close up of the Empire State Building, at sunset, with Downtown in the background.

# INTRODUCTION Visions of New York

IN ORDER TO DISCOVER NEW YORK IN ALL ITS IMMENSITY YOU MUST ASCEND, GO UP TO THE PANORAMIC PLATFORM OF THE EMPIRE STATE BUILDING OR ROCKEFELLER CENTER, GET LOST IN THE LABYRINTH OF ITS STREETS AND ALLEYWAYS, IN ITS WORLD OF WATER AND STONE, INTERRUPTED BY ISLANDS OF GREENERY, IN A PHANTASMAGORICAL KALEIDOSCOPE OF THOUSANDS OF LIGHTS IN TIMES SQUARE, AND CATCH A GLIMPSE OF THE STATUE OF LIBERTY, WHICH, AS IN THE PAST, EMERGES FULL OF PROMISE FOR THE FUTURE. NEW YORK OFFERS A GREAT VARIETY OF VIEWS, SIGHTS AND PANORAMAS THAT CAN FADE AWAY OR CHANGE AT EVERY BLOCK.

THERE ARE THE MORE TYPICAL SIGHTS OF THE CITY SUCH AS THE BATTERY PARK AREA, CONSISTING OF THE PARK AND TALL APARTMENT HOUSES WHERE MANY MANAGERS LIVE. BEHIND THIS IS THE FINANCIAL DISTRICT WITH WALL STREET; THE FEDERAL HALL; THE NEW YORK STOCK EXCHANGE; BOWLING GREEN; THE FAMOUS BRONZE SCULPTURE OF THE *BOWLING GREEN BULL*; ST. PAUL'S CATHEDRAL, WHERE GEORGE WASHINGTON WORSHIPPED; GROUND ZERO,

## INTRODUCTION Visions of New York

WHERE THE NEW WORLD TRADE CENTER IS UNDER CONSTRUCTION; THE WORLD FINANCIAL CENTER, CITY HALL AND MUNICIPAL BUILDING; AND THE CRIMINAL COURTS BUILDING AND NY COUNTY COURT-HOUSE. THERE IS THE SOUTH STREET SEAPORT, WHICH LIES AROUND THE MARKETPLACE AND PIERS STORES AND SHOPS, OVERLOOKED BY THE BROOKLYN BRIDGE. THERE ARE SIGHTS THAT HARKS BACK TO THE PAST, INCLUDING SUCH HISTORIC CHURCHES AS ST. PAUL'S CATHEDRAL, BUILT IN 1878, AND THE NEO-GOTHIC TRINITY CHURCH, DATING BACK TO 1846... AND THEN THERE ARE THE 'NEW WORLDS' WITH A FUTURISTIC LOOK THANKS TO THE PREVALENCE OF GLASS AND STEEL.

THE PROFILE OF MANHATTAN HAS CHANGED IN RECENT YEARS, SINCE IT HAS BEEN TRANSFORMED BY ECLECTIC ARCHITECTURE AND ORIGINAL AND FUTURISTIC SHAPES THAT ARE COMPLICATED, ELABO-RATE, SPECTACULAR, OR SIMPLY DIFFERENT. A RECURRENT STATE-MENT BY ARCHITECTS IS: "WHY NOT? AFTER ALL, THIS IS NEW YORK, WHERE ONE CAN DO ANYTHING." EXPERIMENTATION HAS THUS EN-

## INTRODUCTION Visions of New York

RICHED THE CITY WITH SEVERAL NEW STRUCTURES – MUSEUMS, SKYSCRAPERS, HOTELS, FOUNDATIONS, AND CULTURAL CENTERS – WHOSE ARCHITECTURE REFLECTS THE NEW CONCEPT OF LIGHT AND GLASS, TEMPERED BY AN ENVIRONMENTAL AWARENESS THAT HAS LED TO THE CREATION OF A GREAT MANY GREEN BUILDINGS. SYMBOLS OF NEW YORK CITY – SUCH AS THE FLATIRON BUILDING, THE EMPIRE STATE BUILDING, THE NEW YORK PUBLIC LIBRARY, THE CHRYSLER BUILDING, AND GRAND CENTRAL STATION – NOW MERGE WITH THE ASYMMETRICAL AND UNDULATING BEEKMAN TOWER DESIGNED BY FRANK GEHRY (2011); THE CONDOMINIUM AT 100 11TH STREET, JEAN NOUVEL'S 'VISIONARY MACHINE' (2010), WHICH IS A MOSAIC OF PANELS AND WINDOWS; THE GREEN PROMENADE DESIGNED BY THE ARCHITECTS DILLER SCOFIDIO + RENTRO AND THE JAMES CORNER FIELD OPERATIONS LANDSCAPE ARCHITECTURE STUDIO, WHICH HAVE TRANSFORMED THE HIGH LINE, THE ABANDONED ELEVATED RAILROAD SPUR, WITH FOUNTAINS, PLANTS, PLAYS OF LIGHT AND INSTALLATIONS; THE TALL BANK OF AMERICA TOWER, MADE OF

## INTRODUCTION Visions of New York

GLASS AND STEEL; THE IAC BUILDING BY FRANK GEHRY, IN THE SHAPE OF A SHIP WITH ITS SAILS UNFURLED... IN ADDITION, THERE ARE THE NEW ACADEMIC BUILDING OF THE COOPER UNION DESIGNED BY THOM MAYNE; THE TICKET BOOTH BY PERKINS EASTMAN, AT DUFFY SQUARE; RENZO PIANO'S NEW YORK TIMES BUILDING; THE HEARST MAGAZINE BUILDING DESIGNED BY SIR NORMAN FOSTER; THE TWO TOWERS OF THE TIME WARNER CENTER CREATED BY DAVID CHILDS; THE RESIDENTIAL BUILDINGS AT PERRY WEST THAT RICHARD MEIER DESIGNED; THE LVMH OF CHRISTIAN DE PORTZAMPARC; THE ENLARGEMENT OF THE MORGAN LIBRARY ON THE PART OF RENZO PIANO; THE COLORFUL WESTIN HOTEL, WHICH LOOKS LIKE A TYPICAL BUILDING IN MIAMI THAT IS LOCATED IN TIMES SQUARE... NEW YORK CONTINUES TO BE INSPIRED BY THE MYTH OF HEIGHT, AS CAN BE SEEN IN THE VISION OF DANIEL LIBESKIND AND MANY OTHER ARCHITECTS OF THE 'NEW WORLD TRADE CENTER', WHICH IS BEING CONSTRUCTED AT GROUND ZERO, AT THE SITE OF THE TERRORIST ATTACK OF SEPTEMBER 11 THAT DESTROYED THE TWIN TOWERS.

*34* ● Ellis Island, the old military arsenal from 1892 to 1954 was the main gateway for immigrants entering the United States. Today it hosts the Ellis Island Immigration Museum. A single ticket enables you to take the ferry to visit the museum and the Statue of Liberty.

*35* ● The Statue of Liberty stands at the entrance of the port on Hudson River, on rocky Liberty Island and is the sight that met immigrants when they reached New York.

The Statue of Liberty is 305 ft (93 m) high, including 154 ft (47 m) of the pedestal. It is a female figure wearing a long toga with a crown on her head, of which the seven rays represent the seven seas and the seven continents.

*38 and 39* ● In one hand the Statue of Liberty holds a torch, symbolizing the eternal fire of liberty, and in the other she clutches a tablet, that bears the date of 4th July 1776, Independence Day.

*40-41* ● This view embraces the whole of Manhattan Island, the primary location of the District of Manhattan.

*42-43* • The 9/11 Memorial, the first part of the new World Trade Center was opened to the public on 12th September 2011. It is a tribute to the victims of the attacks with two square pools where the Twin Towers once stood.

*43* • The two serene reflecting pools are ringed by the names of the victims of the terrorist attacks chiseled in bronze.

*44-45* • Right, Brooklyn Bridge, extends towards the futuristic skyline of the new New York.

*46-47* ● Wall Street is an important road artery in the Financial District of Manhattan, where the permanent headquarters of the New York Stock Exchange are located. Wall Street takes its name from the city walls, now long since gone.

*48* ● The Wall Street Bull is a bronze sculpture by the Sicilian artist Arturo Di Modica, and is located in Bowling Green Park.

*49* ● The New York stock exchange is one of the most famous in the world and its facade is often adorned with a huge stars and stripes flag.

*50-51* ● Brooklyn Bridge and the skyscrapers of Lower Manhattan Financial District, very early in the morning, before the heavy traffic starts.

● One of the most
spectacular places
from which to see
the skyscrapers
of Manhattan is
the Brooklyn Heights
Promenade.

54 • The IAC Building, a Late Modern Deconstructivist construction, designed by the famous architect, Frank Gehry was completed in 2007 in the Chelsea neighborhood.

54-55 • The IAC Building looks like a huge ship in full sail, with its white glass and zinc walls.

The IAC Building is Frank Gehry's first building in New York. It has transparent glass walls through which the offices inside are visible.

• The Westin Hotel looks like something out of Miami, but it is in New York. This brightly colored, original, provocative hotel was completed in 2002 and it marked the rebirth of Times Square.

60 • The Westin Hotel also symbolizes the multi ethnic character of New York; the glass tower and the fusion of blues, pinks and oranges reflect the frenetic pace of the city, like multi-colored domino tiles that recall the traffic and the movement in the area.

61 • The building was designed by Arquitectonica, the Miami based firm of Bernardo Fort-Brescia, originally from Lima, and Laurinda Spear.

• 100 11th street was described by its architect, Jean Nouvel, as a "vision machine." The building was started in 2007 and completed in 2010 and features provocative contrasts between the interior and the exterior, and between intimacy and the urban context. The curtain wall glitters with a mosaic of 1650 different sized panes of colorless glass that boast a spectacular view of the Hudson River and High Line Park.

64-65 ● Thom Mayne, founder of Morphosis Architects, together with Gruzen Samton, was chosen to design Cooper Union's "New Academic Building."

65 ● The new building is ecological, and thanks to its design it exploits 75% of natural light. The external wall panels can be swiveled open or closed individually by remote control.

The famous Statue of Atlas stands in front of the International Building at the Rockefeller Center.

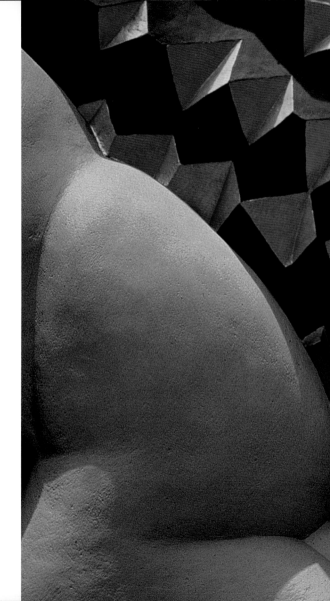

Detail of a decoration
of the Rockefeller
Center, a building that
has always been a
symbol of prestige and
power in New York.

The Statue of Prometheus dominates the heart of the Rockefeller Center.

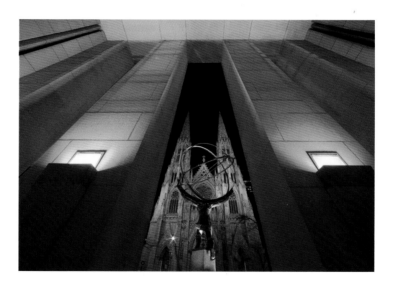

- St. Patrick's Cathedral is the seat of the archbishop of the Archdiocese of New York. It was built between 1853 and 1878 in the decorated Neo-Gothic style of medieval European cathedrals. It stands on the elegant 5th Avenue and is 393,7 ft (120 m) long and 173,8 (53 m) wide and its bell towers are 325 ft (99 m) high.

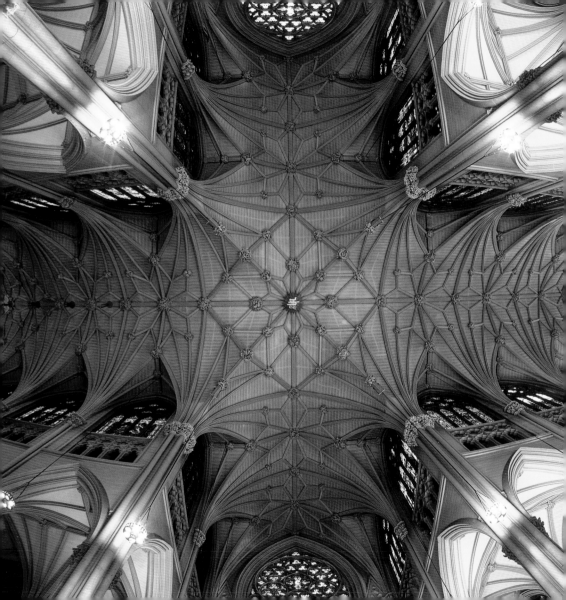

The Grand Central Station is the largest railway station in the world by number of platforms. The clock on the facade is one of the finest examples of Tiffany glass and it is surrounded by sculptures carved by John Donnelly of Minerva, Hercules and Mercury.

The Main Concourse is one of the symbols of New York. The four-faced clock on top of the information booth is perhaps the most famous icon of the station. Each of the four clock faces is made from opal.

78-79 • The New York Times Tower designed by Renzo Piano was built between 2003 and 2007 has been described as a masterpiece of post-modernism.

79 • The 1.200,7 ft (366 m) high Bank of America Tower, designed by Cook + Fox Architects, in One Bryant Park. It was completed in 2009 and is one of the most efficient eco-friendly buildings.

*80-81* ● The General Electric Building, a skyscraper in Art Deco style, is the powerhouse of the Rockefeller Center.

*82-83* ● Times Square, a busy crossroad, famous for the spectacle of lights and billboards glittering from the buildings around it.

84 • 42nd Street is one of the busiest and most famous streets in New York. Grand Central Station and Bryant Park are on this street that also features in many films.

85 • In the streets around Times Square you often see mounted police patrolling the area.

The buildings in Times Square are covered in all sorts of posters, billboards and neon signs that have come to be called "spectaculars."

The Flatiron Building was one of the highest skyscrapers in New York when it was completed in 1902. Newyorkers gave it this name because its shape resembles an iron.

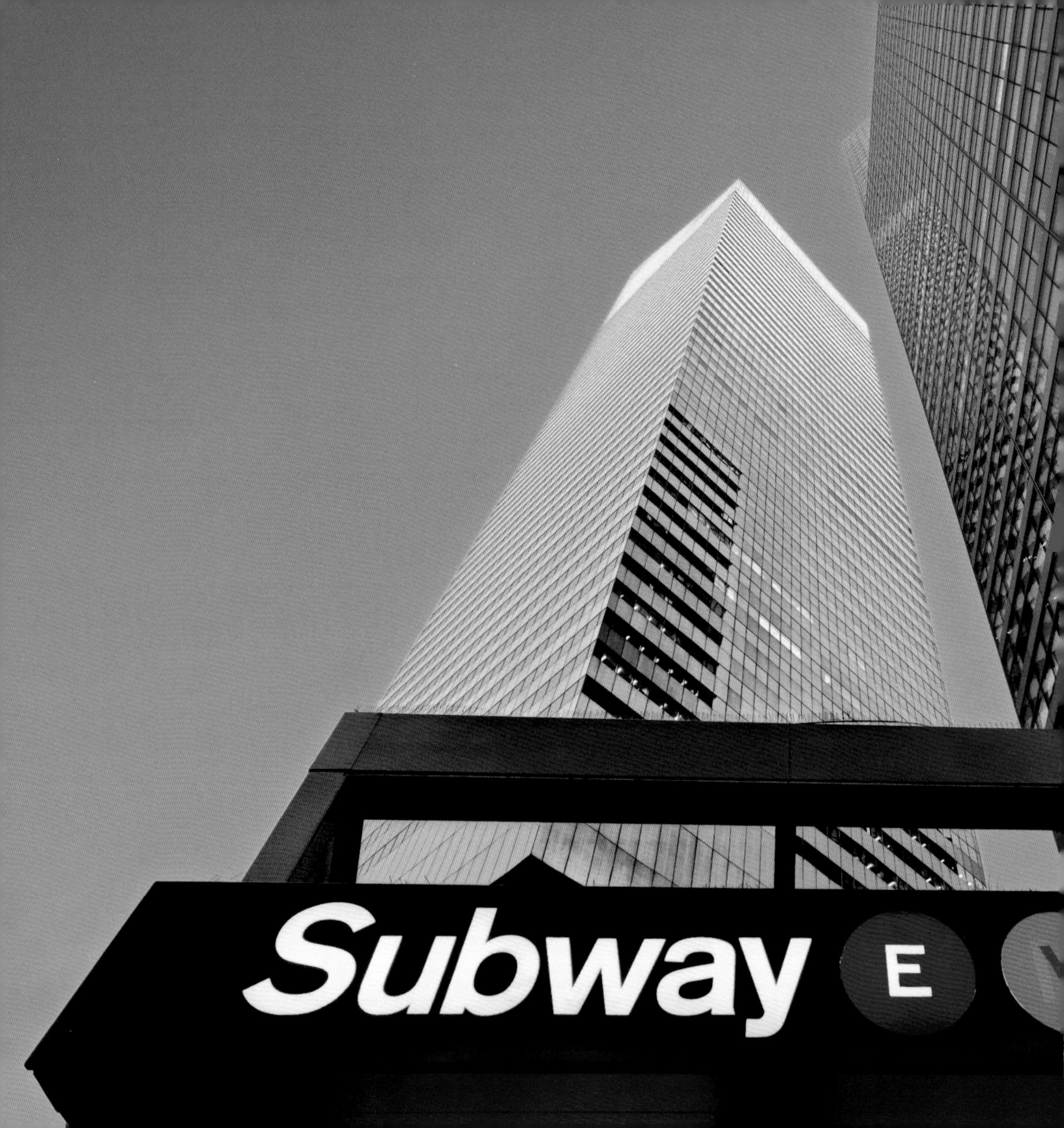
Subway
E

New York City Subway is one of the oldest and most extensive public transport systems in the world, with 468 stations in operation, 229 mi (368,461 km) of passenger routes with a total of 842 mi (1355 km) of track.

92-93 • The center of Midtown is dominated by tall skyscrapers. Right the Empire State Building stands out.

93 • A close up view of the Empire State Building architecture with the Chrysler Building in the background.

94 • In New York the reflection of the skyscrapers on each other create sensational light effects and views. In this picture, you can recognize the Chrysler Building.

95 • The tip of the Chrysler Building is reflected in the glass walls of another very high skyscraper, transforming its shape and colors.

In this unusual view, you can observe one of the gargoyles on the Chrysler Building.

98 • The two towers of the Time Warner Center stretch upwards to the sky opposite the globe of the Trump International Hotel and Tower.

99 • The skyscrapers of Lower Manhattan look onto the river exhibiting their different architectural styles.

The Beekman Tower, designed by Frank Gehry, was completed in 2011. It was immediately described as a "dynamic tower" because of its symmetrical geometric shape. The glass and steel curtain wall reflects the colors of nearby buildings and the changing daylight.

● The New York skyline is one of the most spectacular in the world.

104-105 • The Hearst Magazine Building, the headquarters of the Hearst Corporation, towers over Midtown.

105 • The original six floor building in Art Deco style was refurbished by Sir Norman Foster who was entrusted with the task of building a tower that was started in 2003 and inaugurated in 2006.

*106 and 106-107* • The modern part of the Hearst Building was designed by Norman Foster: it is an entirely ecological structure.

*108-109* • The view embraces the whole of Central Park, 3.4 sq km (1.3 sq mi) of fields, woods, lakes, ponds and playing fields.

# A CITY within the CITY

Detail of a typical Cast-iron house in SoHo.

## INTRODUCTION A City within the City

New York is like an endless onion that one discovers layer upon layer and never gets tired of peeling. Every neighborhood has its very own life and spirit, like a city within the city. Yet they are all connected in their common destiny as members of a single metropolitan entity. But only if you leave behind the surface appearances and delve into the true soul of the less known neighborhoods will you really be able to understand the true spirit of New York City. New York is divided administratively into five districts or boroughs: the island of Manhattan, the Bronx (the only borough separated from Manhattan by the Harlem River), Queens, Brooklyn and Staten Island. Manhattan itself is divided into downtown, midtown and uptown, which in turn consist of various neighborhoods, some of which have only recently taken on their very own identity. New York begins from downtown, the lowest part of Manhattan Island. "In no other city like

## INTRODUCTION A City within the City

NEW YORK DOES DOWNTOWN INDICATE A CULTURAL MICROCOSM IMPLYING A PARTICULAR SENSIBILITY, WHICH ALSO EMBRACES NEW MODERN 'ARTS' RANGING FROM GASTRONOMY TO FASHION, DESIGN AND ALL POSSIBLE FORMS OF EXPRESSION," DECLARED GRAYDON CARTER, DIRECTOR OF *VANITY FAIR* AND CO-OWNER OF THE WAVERLY INN & GARDEN RESTAURANT. LOWER MANHATTAN INCLUDES THE FINANCIAL DISTRICT. CHINATOWN CAN BE RECOGNIZED IMMEDIATELY BY ITS PAGODAS OVER THE SHOPS, BANKS AND MARKETPLACES AND THE SIGNS WRITTEN IN CHINESE. NOT FAR AWAY IS THE BOWERY, THE HISTORIC AND NEWLY GENTRIFIED NEIGHBORHOOD WHOSE NAME DERIVES FROM THE OLD DUTCH WORD FOR 'FARM', *BOUWERIJ*, WHICH HAS REALIZED A COMBINATION OF TRENDY AND UNDERGROUND CULTURES. THE HEART OF LITTLE ITALY IS MULBERRY STREET, CHARACTERIZED BY QUAINT ITALIAN RESTAURANTS, PASTRY SHOPS AND CAFÉS, AND CHURCHES SUCH AS THE CHURCH OF THE MOST PRECIOUS BLOOD AND THE OLD SAINT PATRICK'S CATHEDRAL. THE NEWLY DEVELOPED,

# INTRODUCTION A City within the City

ADJACENT NEIGHBORHOOD KNOWN AS NOLITA IS A FAVORITE WITH MODELS AND ACTORS FOR ITS BOUTIQUES AND MANY DESIGNERS. THE LOWER EAST SIDE IS A HISTORIC LOWER-CLASS, IMMIGRANT NEIGHBORHOOD THAT IN THE PAST CONSISTED MOSTLY OF JEWISH PEOPLE AND IS NOW POPULATED MAINLY BY ASIANS AND HISPANICS: A MULTICULTURAL AREA, AS IS ATTESTED BY SUCH LANDMARKS AS THE LOWER EAST SIDE TENEMENT MUSEUM AND THE SYNAGOGUES. TRIBECA, WITH ITS LOFTS, ART GALLERIES AND PREMIER RESTAURANTS, IS CONSIDERED THE "NEIGHBORHOOD OF ACTOR ROBERT DE NIRO," WHO REVITALIZED IT WITH THE TRIBECA FILMFESTIVAL, THE GREENWICH HOTEL AND THE TRIBECA GRILL AND NOBU RESTAURANTS. SOHO, ONE OF THE MOST STYLISH NEIGHBORHOODS, IS KNOWN FOR ITS CAST-IRON BUILDINGS AND SPECIAL ATMOSPHERE ALONG SPRING STREET, PRINCE STREET, BROOME STREET, AND GREEN STREET. GREENWICH VILLAGE, BETTER KNOWN AS "THE VILLAGE" – CHARACTERIZED BY TREE-LINED AVENUES, COURTYARDS, LOW-RISE APARTMENT HOUSES, WASH-

# INTRODUCTION A City within the City

INGTON SQUARE PARK WITH ITS ARCH, AND THE PUBS AND CLUBS FEATURING LIVE JAZZ – IS A WORLD IN ITSELF MADE POPULAR IN THE LAST CENTURY BY BOHEMIAN ARTISTS AND POETS, AUTHORS, AND INTELLECTUALS, INCLUDING DYLAN THOMAS, MARK TWAIN, HENRY JAMES, JOHN REED, E.E. CUMMINGS, EUGENE O'NEILL, EZRA POUND, T.S. ELIOT, EDGAR ALLAN POE, JACKSON POLLOCK, JACK KEROUAC AND THE UNDERGROUND POETS OF THE BEAT GENERATION. THE EAST VILLAGE HAS A HIPPY ATMOSPHERE AND CONTINUES TO ATTRACT POLITICALLY ENGAGED ARTISTS AND MANY IMMIGRANTS. CHELSEA, WHICH IS POPULAR PARTLY DUE TO THE GAY SCENE AS WELL AS FOR ARTISTS LIKE ANDY WARHOL (WHO MADE THE MOVIE *CHELSEA GIRLS*) WHO LIVED IN THE CHELSEA HOTEL, BOASTS LONG STREETS WITH A GREAT MANY OUTSTANDING GALLERIES. THE MEATPACKING DISTRICT, ONCE FILLED WITH SLAUGHTERHOUSES (ONLY A COUPLE HAVE RE-MAINED) IS NOW THE HIGHLY FASHIONABLE "24-HOUR NEIGHBOR-HOOD," FAMOUS FOR ITS BOUTIQUES AND SHOPS IN THE DAYTIME

# INTRODUCTION A City within the City

AND NIGHT CLUBS IN THE EVENING. MIDTOWN LIES IN THE CENTER OF MANHATTAN AND IS THE BUSINESS AND COMMERCIAL DISTRICT WITH BANKS AND OFFICES AS WELL AS A POPULAR TOURIST AREA. MIDTOWN WEST IS ANIMATED, THANKS TO TIMES SQUARE, THE THEATER DISTRICT AND THE RECENTLY RENOVATED HELL'S KITCHEN, FEATURING DIFFERENT RESTAURANTS AND NIGHTCLUBS. MIDTOWN EAST IS CALMER, WITH AREAS LIKE MURRAY HILL, GRAMERCY PARK AND THE ZONE AROUND THE UNITED NATIONS, WHILE A LIVELY ATMOSPHERE IS TO BE FOUND AGAIN AT HERALD SQUARE AND MADISON SQUARE PARK. MIDTOWN IS POPULAR WITH VISITORS BECAUSE OF ITS MANY ATTRACTIONS: THE EMPIRE STATE BUILDING, THE FLATIRON BUILDING, ROCKEFELLER CENTER, THE CHRYSLER BUILDING, GRAND CENTRAL STATION AND GIGANTIC ST. PATRICK'S CATHEDRAL. UPTOWN IS LOCATED IN THE NORTHERN-MOST PART OF MANHATTAN, AND THE NEW YORK SHOWN IN MANY FILMS DIRECTED BY WOODY ALLEN IS IN THE UPPER WEST SIDE – CHARACTERIZED BY TOWNHOUSES, BROWN SANDSTONE HOMES,

## INTRODUCTION A City within the City

ELEGANT BUILDINGS AND HISTORIC APARTMENTS BUILDINGS LIKE THE MAJESTIC APARTMENTS, THE CENTURY APARTMENTS, THE SAN REMO, ELDORADO AND ANSONIA HOUSE, AND SHOPS AND CAFÉS WITH A DISTINCTIVELY EUROPEAN AIR – AND IN THE UPPER EAST SIDE, WHICH IS MOSTLY RESIDENTIAL AND EXCLUSIVE AND BOASTS MUSEUM ROW, THE PART OF 5TH AVENUE LINED WITH SO MANY MUSEUMS. AGAIN IN THE EAST SECTOR, AT THE CHARMING CARL SCHURZ PARK IS THE GRACIE MANSION, THE RESIDENCE OF THE MAYOR. THE SILK STOCKING DISTRICT, IS A SUCCESSION OF ELITE CLUBS, SYNAGOGUES, PRIVATE SCHOOLS AND ST. DAVID'S UNIVERSITY, WHICH JOHN KENNEDY ATTENDED, AND CHURCHES SUCH AS THE CENTRAL PRESBYTERIAN CHURCH, FREQUENTED BY JOHN D. ROCKEFELLER AND ALL NEW YORK HIGH SOCIETY. HARLEM IS THE AFRICAN-AMERICAN NEIGHBORHOOD OF MUSIC, THE FOCAL POINT OF WHICH IS THE APOLLO THEATER AS WELL AS SEVERAL JAZZ NIGHTCLUBS, AND IT IS ANIMATED BY THE MANY SMALL MARKETS AND THE GOSPELS SUNG IN THE NUMEROUS

CHURCHES. EAST HARLEM DIFFERS IN THAT IT HAS A MARKED HIS-PANIC AND LATINO SPIRIT. IN FACT IT IS POPULATED BY CENTRAL AND SOUTH AMERICAN IMMIGRANTS, AS CAN BE SEEN IN THE EXHI-BITIONS OF THE MUSEO DEL BARRIO. MORNINGSIDE HEIGHTS COM-PRISES THE NEO-GOTHIC CHURCH OF ST. JOHN THE DIVINE, THE NATIONAL MEMORIAL, AND COLUMBIA UNIVERSITY, WHILE THE MARVELOUS CLOISTERS MUSEUM IS SITUATED AT WASHINGTON HEIGHTS. PAST MANHATTAN THERE IS BROOKLYN, WHICH IS DEVEL-OPING INTO A NEW METROPOLIS WITH NEIGHBORHOODS. THERE IS BROOKLYN HEIGHTS, WHERE TRUMAN CAPOTE AND WALT WHIT-MAN LIVED AND DUMBO – AN ACRONYM FOR DOWN UNDER THE MANHATTAN BRIDGE OVERPASS – CONSISTS OF MANY ART GAL-LERIES AND ARTISTS' STUDIOS. THE PARK SLOPE NEIGHBORHOOD, WHICH BOASTS THE BROOKLYN MUSEUM OF ART, IS A FAVORITE WITH AUTHORS SUCH AS PAUL AUSTER, WHO LIVES IN A TOWN-HOUSE A FEW STEPS AWAY FROM PROSPECT PARK. WILLIAMS-BURG IS POPULAR WITH ACTORS AND MODELS BECAUSE OF ITS

## INTRODUCTION A City within the City

CROWDED STREETS OFFERING NEW FASHIONS AND A HOST OF ART GALLERIES, WHILE FORT GREEN, WITH THE BROOKLYN ACADEMY OF MUSIC, AFRICAN RESTAURANTS AND NIGHT CLUBS FEATURING LIVE MUSIC, IS CONSIDERED THE NEW HARLEM. CONEY ISLAND IS STILL FAMOUS FOR ITS AMUSEMENT PARK AND THE RUSSIAN COMMUNITY. QUEENS IS A MAJOR CULTURAL BOROUGH THAT BOASTS THE P.S. 1 CONTEMPORARY ART CENTER AND SEVERAL OTHER MUSEUMS, AS WELL AS A MULTICULTURAL RESIDENTIAL AREA. AND THE BRONX IS UNDERGOING A REVIVAL THANKS TO ITS HIP-HOP MUSICIANS AND A NEWLY DEVELOPED ARTISTS' COMMUNITY. AMONG THE IMPORTANT ATTRACTIONS HERE ARE THE HUGE BRONX ZOO, THE VAST BRONX BOTANICAL GARDEN, EDGAR ALLAN POE'S COTTAGE AND THE ELEGANT RIVERDALE AREA WITH WAVE HILL, WHERE ROOSEVELT, MARK TWAIN AND TOSCANINI LIVED. A SHORT FERRY RIDE TAKES YOU TO STATEN ISLAND, WHICH HAS MANY COLONIAL BUILDINGS AND BREATHES THE AIR OF THE FRENETIC CITY ONLY FROM A DISTANCE.

*120* ● The Chinese dragon appears in the streets of Chinatown during the Chinese New Year celebrations.

*120-121* ● The celebrations are very popular in Chinatown and the streets are always teeming with people at this time of the year.

122-123 • Chinatown continues to grow so that it extends into some parts of of Little Italy.

123 • There are many Chinese food shops and even Chinese pharmacies that offer alternative medicine.

A wedding in Chinatown. Chinese traditions are still very much respected and indeed, many of the residents still speak only Chinese.

126 • Chinese decorations dominate the architecture of the whole of Chinatown, creating a very evocative atmosphere.

126-127 • The streets of Chinatown are mainly frequented by people of Asian origin. It is estimated that the Chinese population of the district is 100,000 but it is difficult to ascertain the exact number.

A view of Little Italy, with a building painted like an Italian flag, advertising the popular Ristorante Puglia. The whole area is full of Italian restaurants and cafés.

● On the Feast of San Gennaro
all the streets of Little Italy are
decorated with the colors of the
Italian flag: red, white, and green.
In the streets, there are artists and
musicians creating a wonderful
folkloristic atmosphere.

132 • The promenade in front of the Ristorante Mela, one of the most popular restaurants in Little Italy.

133 • The famous Da Nico restaurant is an institution in Little Italy and is situated at 164 Mulberry Street, one of the most beautiful streets and also one of the most popular with tourists, in the area.

● Cheeses, hams,
salamis and other
typical cured meats
displayed in the window
of a butcher's shop
in Little Italy.

136 • To the north of Little Italy lies Nolita (North of Little Italy), a fashionable area, where the streets are full of shops.

137 • The Vesuvio Bakery is a meeting place in the very popular district of West Village. There are also many Italian restaurants, confectioneries and bakeries in this area as many people of Italian origin live there.

160 · VESUVIO BAKERY · 160
ITALIAN BREAD
& BISCUITS
VESUVIO
BAKERY
ZAGAT
RATED
CAFE
Experienced Counter
Help Wanted

138-139 ● A cyclist dressed in a traditional British costume participates in the Tweed Run, started by Rugby Ralph Lauren in Greenwich Village.

139 ● Characteristic little houses line the streets of Greenwich Village, where sometimes it looks as though time has stopped.

The statue of General Philip Henry Sheridan, a hero of the Civil War, stands in Christopher Park, in West Village.

*142* ● Greenwich Village is characterized by quiet streets lined with old townhouses. Here, you feel as if you were in another world, far away from the city traffic.

*142-143* ● In Perry Street and in other nearby streets, houses are often fronted by lush green gardens.

● At the Hercules
Fancy Grocery, at
27 Morton Street, in
Greenwich Village, you
find food, fruit and
vegetables but also a
wide selection of beer.

ERCULES FANCY GROCERY
27½ MORTON ST.
GROCERY STORE
(212) 929-6546
BUD LIGHT
OPEN
BROOKLYN
"Hercules Fancy Grocery"
BEER HOLDER
FIRE LOGS
COLD BEER

146 • This clothes shop sits in the middle of the picturesque houses of Greenwich Village, where both new and famous designers have opened boutiques.

147 • Street art is increasingly popular in New York. It is still regarded as vandalism by the authorities but it continues to proliferate in many areas of the city.

148 • These buildings are in one of the most lively areas of the Meatpacking District, formerly a neighborhood where several slaughterhouses were located. The buildings that were once warehouses now host restaurants and trendy nightclubs.

149 • A bridge links some buildings of the Meatpacking District, that have been completely refurbished and now house the ateliers of famous artists and photographers, including Fabrizio Ferri, who has his "headquarters" in this neighborhood.

150 • The gilded statue of Puck on the Puck Building, one of SoHo's historic buildings, built between 1885 and 1886.

150-151 • Many houses in the SoHo neighborhood feature a fire escape staircase. They are still the safest way to escape danger in many old dwellings.

*152-153* ● In New York apartments are so small that people tend to live outside as much as possible, as on these cast iron fire escape stairs in SoHo.

*154-155* ● This famous graffito of Keith Haring is on Houston Street, in the emerging neighborhood of Bowery.

This sculpture entitled "Lunchtime on a Skyscraper," is often displayed in SoHo.

● These are typical houses of the SoHo area along Prince Street. In this neighborhood there is the highest number of buildings with cast iron facades.

The Blue Ribbon Bakery is one of the most fashionable bakeries in SoHo. In this area, even the grocery stores are elegant and refined.

*162-163* ● Over the last few years, many buildings have been constructed in Tribeca: offices, but also many luxury residential apartments.

*163* ● Megu Restaurant, at 62 Thomas Street, in the Tribeca neighborhood offers Japanese cuisine in a very modern setting.

● A foot bridge
connects two lofts
in Tribeca. The
neighborhood is
famous for its beautiful
lofts with high ceilings.

166 • Tribeca boasts the apartments with the highest rents in Manhattan: here traditional architecture blends harmoniously with modern styles.

167 • This contemporary work of art is located opposite the Citigroup Bank in Lower Manhattan. Banks and other large corporate groups often purchase works of art that they use to decorate the interiors and the exterior of their buildings.

Harlem, once considered a very dangerous area, is now enjoying a revival. Indeed, many business men are now moving into the townhouses that they originally bought exclusively as an investment.

*170-171* • This graffito represents life in Harlem.

*172-173* • A graffito on the wall of a building in one of the more fashionable areas in Harlem.

*174-175* ● Malcom X Boulevard in Harlem is one of the most popular streets both with locals and tourists. There are many exotic shops and kiosks, and many examples of large brightly colored graffiti.

*176-177* ● This graffito, again in Harlem, represents the jazz tradition. The whole neighborhood is enjoying a revival. It is also famous for its Sunday Gospel services and for soul food.

*178* • A band of musicians performs in Cadman Plaza in Brooklyn, one of the most residential areas in New York.

*179* • From River Café, under the Brooklyn Bridge, in Brooklyn, you can admire the whole Manhattan skyline. It is one of the most romantic restaurants in New York where many marriage proposals have been made.

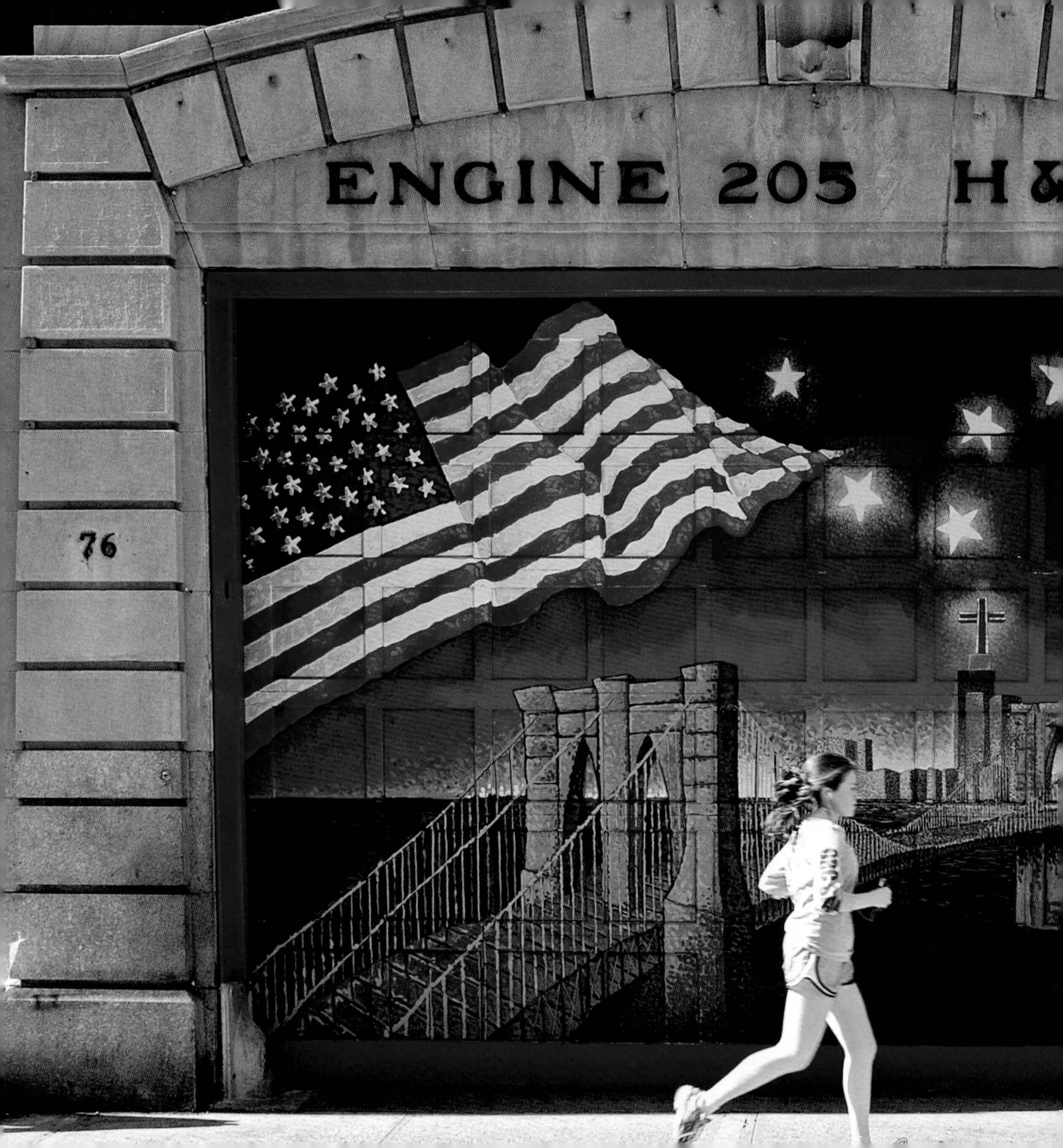
ENGINE 205 H&
76

● This graffito is on the entrance door to the Fire Station in Brooklyn Heights, one of the most beautiful areas in Brooklyn.

**182** • This graffito is on Bedford Avenue in the emerging and very fashionable neighborhood of Williamsburg in Brooklyn.

**182-183** • Queens is currently one of the districts enjoying the greatest revival in New York, with its multi ethnic character and its rents that are still affordable.

● The Al Capone cigar shop in Little Italy in the Bronx at the Arthur Avenue Market, one of the most beautiful and lively areas of the neighborhood.

# ART CAPITAL

# of the WORLD

● The entrance to the Guggenheim Museum, designed by Frank Lloyd Wright, founded in 1937.

## INTRODUCTION Art Capital of the World

New YORK CITY IS THE CULTURAL CAPITAL OF NORTH AMERICA, THE TEMPLE OF CULTURE IN ALL ITS MANIFESTATIONS AND FORMS. THE CITY BOASTS 150 MUSEUMS, AND THE NUMBER IS ALWAYS INCREASING. THERE ARE MORE THAN 400 ART GALLERIES. THERE IS BROADWAY AND ITS MUSICALS AND THE THEATER DISTRICT WITH OPERA AND THEATER, AS WELL AS THE INDEPENDENT OFF-BROADWAY THEATER. THE CITY HAS MANY PRESTIGIOUS UNIVERSITIES, INCLUDING COLUMBIA AND NEW YORK UNIVERSITY, AS WELL AS CULTURAL CENTERS, BOOKSTORES AND LIBRARIES, THE MOST IMPORTANT OF WHICH ARE THE NEW YORK PUBLIC LIBRARY AND THE MORGAN LIBRARY. ANOTHER FACET OF THE LOCAL CULTURE ARE THE HISTORIC PRIVATE CLUBS SUCH AS THE NATIONAL ARTS CLUB, THE EXPLORERS CLUB, AND THE PLAYERS' CLUB, WHERE THERE IS AN ATMOSPHERE OF TIMES GONE BY AMONG ECCENTRIC CHARACTERS, ART COLLECTORS, ARTISTS AND SCIENTISTS.

## INTRODUCTION Art Capital of the World

THE ART GALLERIES CONTINUE TO FLOURISH, AND, BESIDES SO-HO AND CHELSEA, THEY CAN BE FOUND AS FAR AWAY AS IN BROOKLYN, WILLIAMSBURG AND DUMBO, AND ARE NOW SPREADING TO NEW AREAS IN LONG ISLAND AND QUEENS. EXAMPLES OF GALLERIES THAT SET THE LATEST TRENDS ARE THE SPERONE WESTWATER GALLERY OF NORMAN FOSTER AND THE FORBES GALLERIES, WHICH HOUSE THE PERSONAL COLLECTION OF MALCOLM FORBES AT MACMILLAN PUBLISHING AND FEATURE ROTATING EXHIBITIONS.

THE MOST IMPORTANT GRAND CULTURAL 'CATHEDRALS' ARE THE GUGGENHEIM MUSEUM; THE METROPOLITAN MUSEUM OF ART; THE MUSEUM OF MODERN ART (MOMA), RESTRUCTURED IN A SUPER-MODERN FORM BY YOSHIO TANIGUCHI; THE WHITNEY MUSEUM OF AMERICAN ART, AN OFFSHOOT OF THE GALLERY OF MILLIONAIRE ARTIST GERTRUDE VANDERBILT WHITNEY; THE NEUE GALERIE NEW YORK OF GERMAN AND AUSTRIAN

## INTRODUCTION Art Capital of the World

ART AND DESIGN; THE NATIONAL ACADEMY OF DESIGN AND SCHOOL OF FINE ARTS, ESTABLISHED IN 1825 WITH THE AIM OF PROMOTING ART INDEPENDENT FROM ECONOMIC POWER; AND THE PRESTIGIOUS COOPER-HEWITT NATIONAL DESIGN MUSEUM. MANY OF THE MUSEUMS HAVE ALSO REPRESENTED THE ARCHI-TECTURAL AND METROPOLITAN EVOLUTION OF THE CITY. ONE OF THESE IS THE NEW MUSEUM, A STATE-OF-THE-ART STRUC-TURE DESIGNED BY THE JAPANESE ARCHITECTS SEJIMA AND NISHIZAWA THAT SPECIALIZES IN MODERN AND CONTEMPO-RARY ART AND THAT HAS EVEN CONTRIBUTED TO THE REVIVAL OF THE BOWERY NEIGHBORHOOD. THE REMODELING AND EX-PANSION OF THE MUSEUM OF ARTS AND DESIGN (MAD) – CON-CEIVED BY THE ALLIED WORKS ARCHITECTURE STUDIO AND MARKING THE DEBUT OF ARCHITECT BRAD CLOEPFIL – HAS LENT AN ULTRAMODERN AIR TO COLUMBUS CIRCLE. THIS STRUCTURE OPENS OUT DRAMATICALLY, BECOMING FILLED

# INTRODUCTION

WITH NATURAL LIGHT AND OFFERING A MARVELOUS VIEW OF CENTRAL PARK. THE ROSE CENTER FOR EARTH AND SPACE IS A GIGANTIC GLASS CUBE WITH A PLANETARIUM THAT HAS TRANSFORMED THE CLASSIC PROFILE OF THE AMERICAN MUSEUM OF NATURAL HISTORY, ONE OF THE LARGEST NATURAL HISTORY MUSEUMS IN THE WORLD, FAMOUS FOR ITS HUGE DINOSAUR SKELETONS. THEN THERE ARE UNIQUE SPECIALIST MUSEUMS, INCLUDING THE NATIONAL MUSEUM OF THE AMERICAN INDIAN, WHICH HOUSES GEORGE GUSTAV HEYE'S COLLECTION OF NATIVE AMERICAN CULTURE IN A SPLENDID BUILDING CONSTRUCTED IN 1907, THE ALEXANDER HAMILTON U.S. CUSTOM HOUSE; THE MUSEUM OF JEWISH HERITAGE, FEATURING JEWISH ART AND TRADITIONS; THE AMERICAN FOLK ART MUSEUM, HIGHLIGHTING TRADITIONAL AND MODERN FOLK ART; THE ASIA SOCIETY AND MUSEUM, WITH JOHN D. ROCKEFELLER III'S COLLECTION OF ASIAN ART. THE LNTERNATIONAL CENTER OF PHOTOG-

# Art Capital of the World
## Introduction

RAPHY IS THE PIVOTAL POINT OF WORLD PHOTOGRAPHY. IF YOU ARE INTERESTED IN THE ROOTS OF NEW YORK THERE ARE MANY INSTITUTIONS WELL WORTH A VISIT: THE NEW YORK HISTORICAL SOCIETY; THE FRICK COLLECTION, WHICH, BESIDES A MAGNIFICENT COLLECTION OF INTERNATIONAL MASTERS, ALSO INCLUDES MRS. FRICK'S BEDROOM; THE MUSEUM OF THE CITY OF NEW YORK; AND THE SOUTH SEAPORT MUSEUM, WHICH FEATURES THE HISTORY OF THE HARBOR, INCLUDING THE ADVENTURES OF OLD-TIME SAILORS AND HISTORIC SHIPS SUCH AS THE *PEKING, WAVERTREE, PIONEER* AND *AMBROSE*, WHICH ARE STILL ANCHORED AT THE PIERS. NEW YORK CITY IS ALSO THE CAPITAL OF MUSIC – JAZZ, ROCK, BLUES AND OTHER GENRES – AS WELL AS OF DANCE, AS IS ATTESTED BY SUCH GRAND INSTITUTIONS AS THE LINCOLN CENTER, CARNEGIE HALL AND THE NIGHT CLUBS IN HARLEM.

- "La Rotunda" is situated at the center of the US Customhouse inside the National Museum of the American Indian.

*194* • The Metropolitan Museum of Art, often referred to as "The Met," is one of the biggest and most important museums in the world.

*194-195* • The Met's permanent collection boasts more than two million works of art, divided into nineteen sections. Lessons for children and schools are also held here.

196-197 • Works dating back to Classical Antiquity and Ancient Egypt, paintings and sculptures by almost all the great European Masters and a vast collection of American and Modern Art are permanently on show at the Met.

197 • The Met's collection of Greek and Roman art boasts more than 35,000 works. The museum also has a significant number of African and Asian works as well as works from Oceania and Byzantine and Islamic works.

198 • The Met's collection of Egyptian art includes 36,000 artifacts ranging from the Paleolithic Era to the period of Roman domination.

199 • The great Temple of Dendur was donated to the United States by the Egyptian government in 1965 and in 1978 it was reconstructed in the Sackler Wing of the Met. It is now one of the Museum's main attractions.

The enormous glass facade of the Metropolitan Museum of Art reflects some of the buildings on Upper East Side.

The Museum of Modern Art (MoMA), situated in Midtown, has been re-designed and refurbished, with the addition of a lot of glass, by the Japanese architect Yoshio Taniguchi.

• In the garden of the MoMA there are various sculptures, exhibits and works of Modern Art.

*206 and 206-207* ● The museum collection offers an incredible vision of Modern and Contemporary world Art.

*208-209* ● The MoMA collection includes architectural designs, designer objects, drawings, paintings, sculptures, photographs, serigraphs, illustrations, films and multi media works.

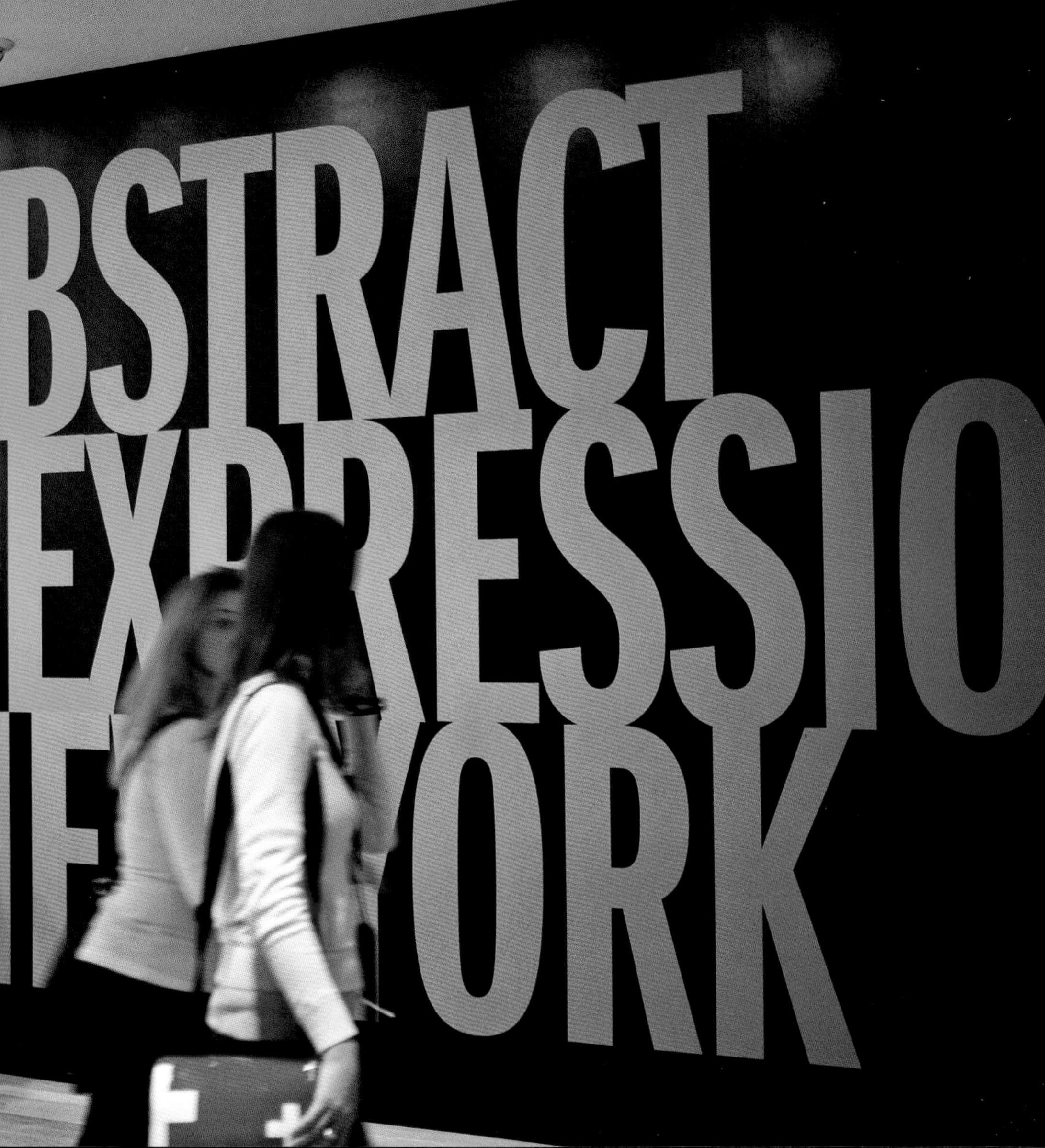
BSTRACT
EXPRESSIO
ORK

*210* • The refurbishing of the MoMA has almost doubled the exhibition areas by adding almost 625,000 sq ft (58,000 sq m) of new space.

*210-211* • "Les Demoiselles d'Avignon" by Pablo Picasso is on display at the MoMA.

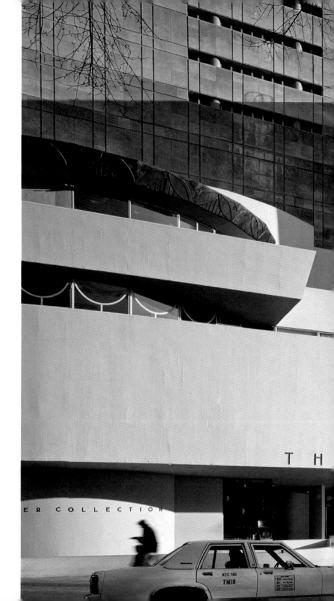

The Guggenheim
Museum stands on 5th
Avenue. The stretch of
road towards Central
Park is known as the
Museum Mile because
many museums are
located there.

Inside the Guggenheim, the gallery is a spiral ramp that rises gently from the ground floor to the top of the building. The paintings are displayed along the walls of the spiral and in some adjacent rooms.

This incredible exhibit was created by the Italian artist Maurizio Cattelan in 2011.

218-219 • The dinosaur collection, at the American Museum of Natural History, includes gigantic dinosaur skeletons, one of the major attractions for adults and children alike.

219 • The American Museum of Natural History is one of the major science and natural history museums in the world.

220 • A scale model of a blue whale hangs from the ceiling of the Hall of Ocean Life at the American Museum of Natural History.

221 • The Globe at the Rose Center for Earth and Space is lit up at night, creating a spectacular effect. It is part of the American Museum of Natural History and includes the Planetarium.

222-223 • The oldest part of the interior of the Morgan Library that dates back to 1902. The library was designed by McKim, Mead and White Architects. It houses a wealth of rare manuscripts, prints and books that are among the most precious in the world.

223 • The Pierpont Morgan Library was expanded and enhanced by the architect Renzo Piano with this new wing.

The New York Public Library is the third largest library in North America and one of the most important in the world.

226 • The American Folk Art Museum in Park Avenue hosts many exhibitions such as "Infinite Variety: three centuries of red and white quilts."

227 • Some visitors at the "Infinite Variety" exhibition, which took place during the Armory Show, an art fair, in March 2011, one of the major city events.

228-229 • The Lincoln Center for the Performing Arts, is a collection of buildings, cinemas and theaters that is home to twelve performing arts organizations.

● The Metropolitan
Opera, is situated
in the Lincoln Center
complex.

232 • At the Museum of Arts and Design, at 2 Columbus Circle you can view this work by Andreas Kocks.

233 • The Museum of Arts and Design has contributed to changing the architectural face of Columbus Circle.

234-235 ● Visitors walking round the exhibits at the "Carsten Holler: experience," on display at the New Museum in December 2011.

235 ● The New Museum of Contemporary Art has the objective of presenting contemporary art from all over the world.

236-237 • The Museum of Jewish Heritage, inaugurated in 1997, is dedicated to the victims of the Holocaust.

237 • In this view, it is possible to distinguish the Museum of Jewish Heritage, situated in the Battery Park complex. The museum was designed by Roche-Dinkeloo and is topped by a pyramid structure called "The Living Memorial to the Holocaust."

*238* ● Brooklyn Museum is the second largest museum in New York and one of the largest in the United States.

*238-239* ● The Entrance Pavilion and Plaza of the Brooklyn Museum. This is where school trips often assemble.

A street in SoHo, teeming with many different modern and contemporary art galleries and designer shops.

*242* • One of the most fashionable streets in SoHo, with boutiques and galleries. Prince Street, Spring Street, Mercer Street, Greene Street and Broome Street are some of the most fashionable streets.

*242-243* • The interior of a furniture and design shop in Broome Street.

• At SICIS, the Art Mosaic Factory, the store is also an atelier. Mosaics that are like works of art are exhibited here, such as these portraits of young girls inspired by models from the 60s.

246 • The Mimi Ferzt Gallery in SoHo, on Greene Street, features contemporary Russian art.

246-247 • Exhibition areas in the Deitch Projects Gallery in Wooster Street, with works by Brazilian artists known as "Os Gemeos" (the twins): Gustavo and Otavio Pandolfo.

# A MOSAIC of FACES

Street artists and tourists inspired by the Statue of Liberty, pose in Battery Park.

## INTRODUCTION A Mosaic of Faces

WHAT IS NEW YORK CITY IF NOT ITS PEOPLE: ANGLO-SAXONS, CHINESE, ITALIANS, JAPANESE, INDIANS, MALAYSIANS, AFRICAN-AMERICANS, FRENCH, JEWS, COLOMBIANS, RUSSIANS, BRAZILIANS, JAMAICANS, SPANISH, HAITIANS... ALL THE NATIONALITIES AND COLORS IN THE WORLD (THERE ARE OVER 8 MILLION INHABITANTS IN NEW YORK CITY, WITHOUT COUNTING THE OUTLYING URBAN AREAS, AND THE POPULATION IS EXPECTED TO REACH 9.5 MILLION BY 2030). THE BIG APPLE IS AN INCREDIBLE MELTING POT OF CULTURES, RELIGIONS, TRADITIONS AND CUSTOMS. YOU IMMEDIATELY FEEL YOU ARE A NEW YORKER, BECAUSE ALL IT TAKES TO BE ONE IS TO LIVE THERE. THE YOUNG MAN FROM THE MIDWEST WHO HAS JUST GRADUATED FROM UNIVERSITY AND GOES TO WALL STREET TO WORK IN THE FINANCIAL WORLD IS A NEW YORKER, AS IS THE ARGENTINE MODEL GETTING READY FOR A SERIES OF PHOTOGRAPHS ON A STREET IN SOHO. THE CHINESE WHO DEAL IN MEDICINAL HERBS AND THE JAPANESE WHO PREPARE SUSHI AT THE COUNTER OF A FASHIONABLE RESTAURANT, ARE ALSO NEW YORK-

## INTRODUCTION A Mosaic of Faces

ERS. THE PUERTO RICAN MESSENGER BOY WHO LIVES IN EAST HARLEM, THE MEXICAN WHO WORKS AS A DOORMAN IN AN ELEGANT BUILDING IN THE UPPER EAST SIDE, THE EUROPEAN WHO RUNS AN ART GALLERY IN THE WILLIAMSBURG NEIGHBORHOOD, THE FAMOUS GERMAN ARCHITECT ABOUT TO INAUGURATE A NEW SKYSCRAPER IN MIDTOWN, THE MOVIE STAR WHO HAS CHOSEN TO LIVE IN MANHATTAN BECAUSE IT IS THE ONLY PLACE IN THE WORLD WHERE NO ONE BOTHERS HER – ALL THESE PERSONS ARE REAL NEW YORKERS. NEW YORK IS THE EYES OF THE NEW YORKERS, BE THEY OLD OR YOUNG, WHO HAVE ALWAYS BEEN ITS VITAL FORCE. NEW YORK IS ALSO ITS STREETS, BECAUSE IT IS THERE THAT PEOPLE MEET AND GET AROUND. THE STREETS MIRROR THE SOUL AND BREATH OF THE CITY – ON THE SIDEWALKS, IN THE STREET LIFE, AT THE NEIGHBORHOOD STREET CORNERS, IN THE WINDOWS OF THE DELICATESSENS WHERE PAKISTANIS, INDIANS AND CHINESE WORK, IN THE RESTAURANTS AND DINERS THAT ARE THE HEART OF THE EVERYDAY LIFE THAT MAKES NEW YORK A VARIEGATED NETWORK

## **INTRODUCTION** A Mosaic of Faces

OF MICROCOSMS. THE STREETS AND AVENUES ALSO HAVE DIFFER-ENT PERSONALITIES - FIFTH AVENUE WITH ITS SHOPS AND TOURIST ATTRACTIONS AND MADISON AVENUE WITH ITS ELEGANT BOU-TIQUES. BROADWAY, AN ARTERY THAT RUNS THROUGH VARIOUS NEIGHBORHOODS AND METROPOLITAN IDENTITIES, AND 42ND STREET, REPRESENTED IN SO MANY FILMS, WHICH RUNS FROM THE HUDSON RIVER TO TIMES SQUARE, BRYANT PARK, GRAND CENTRAL STATION, AND UP TO THE EAST RIVER AND THE UN SECRETARIAT BUILDING, WHERE THERE ARE SO MANY DIFFERENT TYPES AND LAY-ERS OF HUMANITY, AS WELL AS SOME OF THE LEADING ATTRAC-TIONS - BLEECKER STREET, KNOWN FOR ITS STORES, BOOKSHOPS, CAFÉS AND SMALL RESTAURANTS THAT ARE AN INTEGRAL PART OF THE UNIQUE WORLD OF GREENWICH VILLAGE; CANAL STREET AND ITS STALLS OFFERING FAKE OBJECTS, AND CHINESE SHOUTING IN THE STREET TO LURE PASSERS-BY TO MAKE AN IMPULSE PUR-CHASE' COLUMBUS AVENUE, WITH ITS EUROPEAN-TYPE CAFÉS, SYMBOLS OF THE VIVACIOUS LIFE IN THE UPPER WEST SIDE; ST.

# INTRODUCTION A Mosaic of Faces

MARK'S PLACE IN EAST VILLAGE, THE HAUNT OF ROCK MUSICIANS, ANIMATED BY A HODGEPODGE OF RESTAURANTS AND SHOPS MUCH LIKE A BAZAAR; CENTRAL PARK WEST, WHERE MANY ACTORS AND OTHER CELEBRITIES LIVE IN ELEGANT CONDOS AND OLD BUILD-INGS, INCLUDING THE DAKOTA BUILDING, WHERE JOHN LENNON WAS ASSASSINATED. NEW YORK LIFE IS REVEALED IN ITS STREETS. NEW YORK IS ALSO THE NIGHT, WHICH SPARKLES AND THROBS WITH PEOPLE AND THE COLORS OF THOUSANDS OF LIGHTS. FROM THE ANIMATED NIGHT LIFE IN THE CLUBS IN THE MEATPACKING DISTRICT, TO THE BARS IN MIDTOWN, THE PUB AND DIVE BARS IN EAST VILLAGE AND THE LOWER EAST SIDE, FROM THE RESTAURANTS AND THE NIGHT CLUBS FEATURING LIVE MUSIC IN THE WEST VILLAGE TO THE MORE SOPHISTICATED ONES IN SOHO AND TRIBECA – THE CITY "NEV-ER SLEEPS", NEVER DRAWS BREATH. THE VIBRANT RHYTHM OF THE NIGHTLIFE DOMINATES THE STREETS THAT, EVEN IN THE WEE HOURS, ARE STILL FULL OF PEOPLE, JUST AS THE SKYSCRAPERS TAKE ON A VAST GAMUT OF COLORS AT NIGHTFALL.

254 • A manager in the Wall Street area calls a taxi in the street.
Taxis are available when the sign is lit up.

255 • Two lawyers talk at the Supreme Court. New York
is one of the cities with the highest number of lawyers in the world.

● Firemen having a break in Times Square. After 9/11 firemen are considered as true heroes in New York.

A manager has his shoes cleaned in Wall Street opposite the Trinity Church cemetery. All along the street there are shoe shiners of all nationalities.

260 • Delis often stay open twenty-four hours a day.

261 • This street vendor has chosen Downtown to sell his hot dogs but similar street vendors are found all over New York.

**duane** **DR** **rade**

OPEN
24
HOURS

SABRETT
SABRETT
U.S.
GOV'T
INSPECTED
WE'RE ON A ROLL !!!
SABRETT
SABRETT

H&M
UPTOWN. MIDTOWN.
DOWNTOWN.

Hot Dog
Hot Sausage
Hot Pretzel
COLD
Soda, Water & Snapple

SABRETT
Big Apple Pretzel

PEPSI

SABRETT

PEPSI    PEPSI

Hot Dog        Hot Dog
Sausage        Sausage
Hot Pretzel    Hot Pretzel
COLD
Soda, Water & Snapple

SAUSAGE

A street vendor selling bubble blowers in Midtown. New York is the city for business and many people "try their luck" by selling different types of products.

A juggler in Times Square performs in front of a seated audience in a pedestrian zone.

*266* • An artist paints a picture of skyscrapers in the Financial District.

*267* • A craftsman and artist sells his wares and creations on
the sidewalk of a SoHo street.

*268-269* • The Félix Restaurant, currently one of the trendiest places in SoHo,
is a meeting place for elegant and fashionable Newyorkers.

Restaurant

*270* • Italian ice cream parlors are very popular in New York, like the one in the picture with its rather inviting name: "Dolce Vizio Tiramisù."

*270-271* • A salesgirls and a salesman at the "Dolce Vizio Tiramisù" ice cream parlor at the counter where there are various flavors of ice cream, just like in Italy.

Citrus
Sauce

Amaretti

Mixed Nuts

Dark
Chocolate

Dried
Pineapple

Strawberries

Pistachios

Granola

Dried
Coconut

Apricots

Fo
Berr

272 • There are many Starbucks cafés in New York and, Newyorkers love them because they are an ideal meeting place.

272-273 • A young man prepares coffee in a Starbucks café. You order and pay at the cash register and then you queue to collect your drink.

Young people, on the street in the Bronx District find a way to cool off and and have fun in the spray from a fire hydrant.

● Horse-drawn carriages in Central Park are as much loved by tourists as they are by romantic Newyorkers. Many carriages are in the park near the Hotel Plaza.

A street actress and artist performs and improvises in the street in front of children in the charming Washington Square Park in Greenwich Village.

280 ● Vanderbilt Playground in Prospect Park, is considered the Central Park of Brooklyn. The neighborhoods nearby are residential and very popular with families.

281 ● Riders cross Prospect Park in Brooklyn, where horse riding is very popular.

● The Pro Skateboarder Brandon Westgate Competition for the Maloof Money Cup 2011 took place in Flushing Meadows Park in Queens. This is one of the most well-known competitions for this sport and it is very popular with New York teenagers.

● Breakdancers perform in Central Park in front of a crowd. Sometimes you can come across organized shows.

*286-287* • A jogger runs across Brooklyn Bridge, a favorite spot for this sport.

*287* • The Jacqueline Kennedy Onassis Reservoir, reflecting the buildings of Upper West Side, is another favorite jogging track for Newyorkers. It has featured in many films including "Marathon Man" starring Dustin Hoffman.

288 • Roller blade enthusiasts are found in all of the city neighborhoods.

288-289 • A Newyorker stretching after a long run along the river near Brooklyn Bridge.

*290* • The annual New York Marathon, 26.2 mi (42.195 km) around the five districts of New York City.

*290-291* • A crowd of athletes and participants on Queensboro Bridge which leads to Manhattan.

*292-293* • Composure during the parade on St. Patrick's Day.

● Girls dressed for
the St. Patrick's Day
Parade, celebrated by
all Newyorkers of Irish
descent. On this day,
17th March, the color
green pervades
the city.

*296 and 296-297* • Green hats, wigs and spectacles are all over the streets of New York on St. Patrick's Day, when celebrations in pubs and on the streets continue until late into the night.

*298-299* • Participants in fancy dress at the Gay Pride Parade.

*300-301* • The Mexican Parade along Madison Avenue is an absolute explosion of colors.

*301* • A rather eccentric character dances in the street during the Mexican Parade.

302 ● Macy's Thanksgiving Day Parade.

302-303 ● During the Parade balloons of all shapes and sizes, like this Shrek balloon, are seen on the streets of the City.

304 • A float carrying a very lively turkey during the Thanksgiving Day Parade in Central Park.

305 • A girl waves from a decorated float during Thanksgiving Day Parade, one of the popular events most loved by Newyorkers, adults and children alike.

306 ● A Spiderman balloon during Thanksgiving Day Parade, which is always very up to date with cartoon and film characters of the time.

306-307 ● A gigantic Kung Fu Panda towers above the people and the crowded streets of New York during the Thanksgiving Day Parade.

# The COLORS of the BIG APPLE

- As Woody Allen says, New York wakes up in Spring with a very special energy and a very romantic mood. Above all in Central Park, when the trees in bloom are reflected in the lakes and ponds.

## INTRODUCTION The Colors of the Big Apple

NEW YORK IS ALSO THE CITY OF SEASONS, WHICH CHANGE COLOR IN A MAGICAL MIRACLE THAT IS REPEATED EVERY YEAR. WINTER IS THE PERIOD OF BLUES, WHEN THE TREES SHED THEIR LEAVES AND RISE UP TO THE SKY WITH THEIR BARE BRANCHES, SPECTRAL SKELETONS OF THEIR FORMER SELVES, AND WHEN THE SNOW ARRIVES AND SNOWSTORMS COVER THE CITY WITH A WHITE MANTLE THAT SLOWS ALL MOVEMENT AND ATTENUATES ALL NOISE. SPRING INVADES THE FLOWER BEDS WITH TULIPS AND OTHER FLOWERS IN A BONA FIDE ERUPTION OF ALL THE NUANCES OF GREEN. THE TREES BLOOM AND ENLIVEN THE STREETS, AND CENTRAL PARK BECOMES PALE WITH WHITE CHERRY BLOSSOMS WHOSE PETALS FALL ON THE PASSERSBY LIKE CLOUDS OF CONFETTI TRANSPORTED BY THE WIND. SUMMER EXPLODES, TABLES ARE PLACED ON

## INTRODUCTION The Colors of the Big Apple

THE SIDEWALKS OUTSIDE THE CAFÉS AND RESTAURANTS, PEOPLE SIT ON THE GRASS IN THE PARKS TO TAKE IN A BIT OF SUN, READ A BOOK OR HAVE A PICNIC, WHILE OTHERS GATHER TO SIP A COCKTAIL ON THE ROOFTOPS. AUTUMN ARRIVES WITH INDIAN SUMMER AND SPLENDID FOLIAGE THAT SETS THE CITY ABLAZE WITH THE REDS, YELLOWS, ORANGES AND BROWNS OF THE TREE LEAVES THAT ARE REFLECTED IN THE POOLS IN THE PARKS. THEN HALLOWEEN APPROACHES AND NEW YORKERS (EVEN THE DOGS) PUT ON MASKS TO PARTICIPATE IN THE GREENWICH VILLAGE PARADE, WHILE CARVED PUMPKINS AND COBWEBS LIE ON THE THRESHOLDS AND WINDOW SILLS OF THE HOUSES AS WELL AS IN THE SHOP WINDOWS, FOR EXAMPLE ALONG BLEECKER STREET AND THE LANES LINED WITH TOWNHOUSES IN THE WEST VILLAGE.

● A passer-by under an umbrella. New York is a city where it rains very often in the Fall and in winter.

● A view of the city
and Downtown
wrapped in mist that
is very common in
winter in New York.

*316* • A school bus picks up children along the snow covered streets.

*317* • When it snows in New York, traffic slows down, especially in Midtown, as we can see here, with Grand Central Station in the background.

*318* • A Newyorker, with bucket and spade, cleaning the streets after a heavy snowfall.

*318-319* • A girl decides to tackle the heavy snow that has just fallen, on skis. Cross-country skiing is popular among Newyorkers in Central Park.

The tree-lined streets of the City become particularly romantic when the snow falls and the atmosphere becomes rather quaint bringing back memories of the past.

*322* • Benches in Central Park are almost completely covered by a thick layer of white snow.

*322-323* • The elegant buildings of Central Park West and Upper West Side look like ghosts looking onto Central Park covered by a blanket of snow and ice.

The famous Literary Walk in Central Park, is even more evocative and romantic in the snow.

In winter, Central Park is transformed into a magical white world and its lakes are completely frozen.

*328* • Magical views of Central Park in winter. A street light comes on in the early evening.

*328-329* • A romantic little bridge, over a small lake that is not yet completely frozen.

*330-331* • The famous ice rink at "The Pond" is framed by the trees of Central Park and the elegant buildings of the Upper West Side.

332 • The Flatiron Building looks onto a snow-covered Madison Square Park.

333 • Cross-country skiing across Brooklyn Bridge, leading from Manhattan to Brooklyn, in winter.

A female skater performs in front of the gilded statue of Prometheus at the Rockefeller Center.

● An enchanting view of Central Park in spring, when the park becomes green again and regains its colors.

● Trees in bloom near
a fountain in Central Park:
a wonderfully romantic
moment.

340 • The lake covered with water-lilies characterizes the Brooklyn Botanical Garden, that fills with color in spring.

341 • The pond and the Japanese Garden in the Brooklyn Botanical Garden offer particularly romantic views.

*342-343* •
A Japanese family
admire the cherry trees
in blossom in the
Japanese Garden
at the Brooklyn
Botanical Garden.

*344-345* • A cherry
tree in blossom near
the lake in Central Park,
with the buildings of
Central Park West and
Upper West Side in
the background.
Newyorkers often have
picnics in this area.

346 • In spring New York turns pink. Trees in blossom in Washington Square Park
in Greenwich Village can be seen in this picture.

347 • The Flatiron Building peeps out from a cherry tree in Madison Square Park.

348 • Green Market in Union Square is very popular in spring and summer when all the seasonal produce is on sale.

349 • City Hall Park in full bloom in spring. The Municipal Building, where all the important civic events of the city are held, can be seen in the background.

*350* • A horse-drawn carriage stops near some cherry trees in Central Park near the Plaza Hotel.

*350-351* • A cherry tree in blossom in Greenwich Village.

It is said that the rocks in Central Park have a special magnetic quality which gives the city its famous energy. This is a picture of a sunny day in the park.

The famous Coney Island Amusement Park is behind the beach at Coney Island. Both the beach and the Amusement Park are always very crowded in summer.

*356* • The large swimming pool in Astoria Park can be seen under the Triboro Bridge in the Queens district, one of the most residential and multi-ethnic districts of New York.

*357* • Battery Park during the Swedish Midsummer Feast, a very popular summer event.

*358-359* • Lifeguards and surfers on the beach at East Hampton, during a charity event. The Hamptons are a very fashionable place, frequented by the New York jet set during summer weekends and social events.

360-361 • The lake in Central Park is transformed by the colors of Fall. The elegant buildings of Upper West Side and the trees are reflected in the water creating spectacular effects.

361 • The lakes in Central Park look bleak, immersed in the surrounding nature.

362 ● The effect of colors in Fall when Central Park becomes a magical kaleidoscope.

363 ● This romantic bridge in Central Park is dotted with trees that are losing their leaves.

364-365 ● The Literary Walk in Central Park in Fall, when the fallen leaves help to reduce the noise.

365 ● A bridge in Central Park covered with the leaves that fall from the trees in Fall.

366-367 ● Belvedere Castle, in the heart of Central Park, in New York, was built in Victorian style in 1869.

# FASHION
# CAPITAL

● Looking for a taxi among the skyscrapers of Midtown after a shopping spree.

# **INTRODUCTION** Fashion Capital

New York is a fantastic "Toyland", a paradise of irresistible temptations where one may very well become a shopping addict, enveloped in an endless whirl of objects and escalators, with the illusion of being able to find a real bargain, in the true spirit of the city. New York is the world capital of fashion, as is demonstrated historically, for example, by the Flatiron District, who's Ladies' Mile was the place to go for upper middle-class women in the late 19th century, and the Garment District or Fashion District, where one can still see delivery persons push mobile clothes hangers filled with articles. Glamour and the latest trends are in the air, thanks to the gold mine of expert artists and designers who come to the city from the four corners of the world in the quest for fortune, but above all for new inspiration. The world of fashion can also be found in the architecture of the skyscrapers and lifestyles here, as

## INTRODUCTION Fashion Capital

WELL AS IN THE BOUTIQUES, SHOPS, MARKETS, AND BOOKSTORES SUCH AS BARNES & NOBLES, WHICH ARE TRUE "CITY SALONS" WITH AREAS WHERE ONE CAN READ BOOKS AND PERIODICALS. FASHION IS ALSO MANIFESTED IN THE SMALL DOGS THAT WEAR THE LATEST MODEL OF LITTLE BOOTS AND COATS ESPECIALLY DESIGNED FOR CANINES. THE DEPARTMENT STORES HERE ARE LEGENDARY. THREE OF THE BEST-KNOWN ARE THE IMMENSE MACY'S, WHICH IS AN INTEGRAL PART OF NEW YORK CITY LIFE WITH ITS FAMOUS THANKSGIVING PARADE AND SPRING FLOWER FAIR; BLOOMINGDALE'S, WHICH BOASTS THE BEST INTERNATIONAL BRAND NAMES AND WHICH IS STILL FREQUENTED BY NEW YORK HIGH SOCIETY; AND SAKS FIFTH AVENUE, FEATURING LUXURY ITEMS, WHOSE FAÇADE IS COVERED WITH LIGHTS DURING THE CHRISTMAS HOLIDAY SEASON. CENTURY 21 IS THE LARGEST OUTLET, OVERFLOWING WITH SHOPPERS, BOTH LOCAL AND TOURISTS, WHERE YOU CAN FIND CLOTHING AND ACCESSORIES DESIGNED BY LEADING STYLISTS AT BARGAIN PRICES. EVERYTHING

# INTRODUCTION Fashion Capital

IN THESE ESTABLISHMENTS IS AUTHENTIC, WHILE IF YOU ARE LOOKING FOR PERFECT IMITATIONS, GO TO CANAL STREET IN CHINATOWN. THEN THERE ARE THE MAIN SHOPPING AVENUES. NATURALLY, THE MOST POPULAR WITH TOURISTS IS 5TH AVENUE, WITH THE GLASS CUBE APPLE STORE THAT SEEMS TO HAVE ARRIVED FROM ANOTHER PLANET AND, JUST OPPOSITE THE HOTEL PLAZA AT CENTRAL PARK, THE LEGENDARY TIFFANY & CO. JEWELRY STORE, THE HUGE TOY STORE F.A.O. SCHWARZ, THE FUTURIST ARCHITECTURE OF THE HIGHLY ELEGANT BOUTIQUE LOUIS VUITTON, THE BARE-CHESTED MODELS POSING AT THE ENTRANCE TO ABERCROMBIE & FITCH... MADISON AVENUE, FROM 57TH STREET TO 79TH STREET, BOASTS A SERIES OF LUXURY BOUTIQUES. EQUALLY ELEGANT, BUT WITH A MORE INTIMATE AND REFINED ATMOSPHERE, IS BLEECKER STREET IN THE WEST VILLAGE, WHERE THE LEADING STYLISTS, SUCH AS MARC JACOBS, COMPETE WITH ONE ANOTHER, SIDE-BY-SIDE WITH CRAFTSMEN'S SHOPS. BUT THE TIMELESS CENTER OF QUALITY SHOPPING IS SOHO, WHOSE

## INTRODUCTION Fashion Capital

ARABESQUE OF STREETS ARE LINED WITH CAST-IRON HOUSES, APPAREL AND DESIGN SHOPS, ART GALLERIES, BOOKSTORES AND PERFUMERIES. THE NEW TRENDS AND FASHIONS EXTEND AS FAR AS THE MEATPACKING DISTRICT – WHICH BOASTS THE BOUTIQUE OF DIANE VON FUERSTENBERG, AN EXAMPLE OF SPECTACULAR ARCHITECTURE, AND THAT OF STELLA MC-CARTNEY – AND NOLITA (NORTH OF LITTLE ITALY), WHERE ELISABETH STREET, MOTT STREET AND MULBERRY STREET ABOUND IN INTERESTING SHOPS. THE MECCA OF BARGAINS, AS THE NEW YORKERS CALL IT, IS THE LOWER EAST SIDE, WITH A STRING OF APPAREL AND ACCESSORIES STORES ALONG ORCHARD STREET AND LUDLOW STREET. THE EAST VILLAGE IS KNOWN AS THE HUB OF VINTAGE, WHICH IS ACCOMPANIED BY KITSCH, MUSIC, THE ESOTERIC AND EXOTIC IN THE INDIAN AND TIBETAN SHOPS, AND THE UNDERGROUND SPIRIT THAT CHARACTERIZES SEVERAL STREETS, SUCH AS LUDLOW STREET. THIS NEIGHBORHOOD ALSO HAS NEW STYLISTS WHO FAVOR AN ECLECTIC APPROACH TO FASHION.

374 • A creative shop window display.
Professional window dressing in New York
is a job for true artists.

374-375 • The Empire State Building
reflected in the window of a boutique.
The whole area is wonderful for shopping.

*376* ● Bloomingdale's is regarded as one of the best stores for quality brands.

*376-377* ● A large billboard advertising the Abercrombie and Fitch brand dominates the street view in Downtown.

*378* ● A sales man advises some customer on the choice of a jewel. New York is full of jewelers. Tiffany on 5th Avenue is one of the most famous.

*378-379* ● Shops in New York, such as Tiffany in the picture, concentrate on exclusivity and quality because they are in a very competitive environment.

● In Trump Tower, on 5th Avenue, one of the most famous shopping streets in the world, there are also the boutiques of the major designers.

382-383 ● This shop window has been decorated with miniatures of the most famous skyscrapers in New York, including the Chrysler Building.

383 ● The Andy Warhol Monument is the work of sculptor Rob Pruitt. It is located at the corner of 18th Street and Broadway in Union Square.

384-385 ● Macy's is the largest store in the world.

On Black Friday, the day after Thanksgiving and the official opening of Christmas shopping, the crowd is overcome by the frenzy of special offers and sales. The interior of Macy's is seen in this picture.

388 • Stella McCartney's luxury shop is in the Meatpacking District. The designer was one of the first to decide to open her boutique here, contributing to the revival of the whole neighborhood.

389 • The shop window of the All Saints shop, with its sewing machines, is stunning. In the Meatpacking District all the boutiques vie to have the most creative shop window displays.

390 • A passer by admires a shop in SoHo, a very popular place for high quality shopping, with designer shops and art galleries.

390-391 • The writing on the shop window says "Tempt me...": it is easy to fall into temptation in New York with so many shopping opportunities that cater for all tastes.

The glass cube at the Apple store is completely lit up at night. The Apple Store on 5th Avenue is open 24 hours a day.

Some customers take the Apple Store spiral staircase but the shop is on the groundfloor.

396 ● In the enormous Lego shop at the Rockefeller Center, there are gigantic exhibits made from Lego: a real Mecca for Lego enthusiasts.

396-397 ● In this large store architecture plays with shapes and mirrors.

Bleecker Street, one of the most fashionable streets in West Village, where there are the shops of all the major fashion designers. The Ralph Lauren shop window can be seen in this picture.

400 ● In the evening the shops of the shopping malls are illuminated, creating magical light and color effects.

401 ● In keeping with the City theme, this Banana Republic shop window displays a reproduction of "The New Yorker," one of the most popular magazines with Newyorkers and intellectuals.

April 17, 1948     THE     Price 20 cents

NEW YORKER

FASHION'S
NIGHT
OUT
SEPT.10
2010
NYC

FEATURING AN EXCLUSIVE
EXHIBITION OF COVERS
FROM THE ARCHIVES OF
*THE NEW YORKER.*

The large Disney Store, opened in Times Square is a true "amusement park" for both adults and children.

# The MAGIC of LIGHT

- The Statue of Liberty stands in front of a myriad of lights of the skyline of Downtown and the Financial District of New York.

## INTRODUCTION  The Magic of Light

THE LIGHT IN NEW YORK CITY IS UNIQUE, WITH A MAGICAL GAMUT OF COLORS THAT DEPEND ON THE VARIABLE SKY AND STRONG WIND. A COLD LIGHT BLUE EARLY IN THE MORNING LIGHT MIST OFTEN RISING FROM THE GROUND IN THE WINTER. WARM AND YELLOW, IRIDESCENT IN THE EVENING, WHILST THE SUN'S RAYS PENETRATE THE OLD BUILDINGS AND TOWNHOUSES. WHITE BLINDING LIGHT PENETRATES IN THE MIDDLE OF THE DAY, WHEN THE SUN STRIKES THE GLASS WINDOWS OF THE HIGH-RISES, ALMOST AS IF CHALLENGING THEIR PRESENCE IN THE SKY. MILD, SUFFUSED AND OBLIGING WHEN CLOUDS COVER THE SKY, LENDING A MILKY HUE WITHOUT SPATIAL OR TEMPORAL CONFINES.

TO HAVE THE BEST VIEW OF DAWN YOU SHOULD HEAD EAST, BEST IF ALONG THE EAST RIVER, AT MIDTOWN, RIGHT IN FRONT OF THE LARGE RED PEPSI COLA SIGN AT LONG ISLAND. EARLY IN THE MORNING THE NEW YORK SKY IS PINK AND THEN TINGED

# INTRODUCTION The Magic of Light

WITH VIOLET HUES THAT SOMETIMES COLOR THE FLEECY CLOUDS, CREATING INCREDIBLY FASCINATING SCENES. THE FIERY SUNSET OVERWHELMS THE CITY WITH INTENSE ORANGES AND REDS THAT MERGE IN A UNIFORM COLOR ON THE HORIZON OR THAT EMERGE AMONG THE UNCONTROLLABLE MASSES OF CLOUDS THAT ON WINDY DAYS SUDDENLY CHANGE THEIR SHAPE AND APPEARANCE IN AN UNPREDICTABLE PLAY OF SHADOWS. IN ORDER TO FOLLOW THE WESTWARD COURSE OF THE SUN AND ITS SPECTACULAR DESCENT BEHIND THE ROOFS OF THE SMALL HOUSES IN BROOKLYN OR THE SKYSCRAPERS AND OTHER BUILDINGS IN NEW JERSEY, YOU CAN STOP AT CERTAIN POINTS ON THE PEDESTRIAN AND BICYCLE PATH THAT RUNS ALONG THE HUDSON RIVER FOR THE ENTIRE LENGTH OF MANHATTAN, FROM THE UPPER WEST SIDE, AT THE CAFÉ IN RIVERSIDE PARK OR OPPOSITE THE TRUMP SKYSCRAPERS, WHERE THE REMAINS OF THE OLD RAILWAY STAND, AND AS FAR

## INTRODUCTION The Magic of Light

AS THE PIERS OF CHELSEA, TRIBECA PARK, THE YACHT HARBOR OF THE FINANCIAL CENTER, UNDER THE BROOKLYN BRIDGE OR AT BATTERY PARK, WHERE THE PROFILE OF THE STATUE OF LIBERTY CAN BE SPOTTED. OR YOU CAN GO UPWARD FOR QUITE A DISTANCE, TO THE VIEWPOINTS OF TALL HIGH-RISES SUCH AS THE EMPIRE STATE BUILDING OR ROCKEFELLER CENTER. ANOTHER POSSIBILITY IS TO WATCH THE SUNSET FROM THE ROOF OF A TOWNHOUSE WITH A PANORAMIC VIEW OF THE CITY. THE SUN CREATES AN UNFORGETTABLE SPECTACLE, UP TO THE BEWITCHING MOMENT WHEN THE CITY LIGHTS TURN ON ONE BY ONE AS THE SKY GRADUALLY BECOMES TOTALLY DARK: NOW, AS IF BY MAGIC, NEW YORK SUDDENLY TURNS INTO THE MYTHICAL "CITY OF A THOUSAND LIGHTS AND COLORS."

AS IS TO BE EXPECTED, THE MOST INTENSE LIGHT IS IN TIMES SQUARE, A VERITABLE CIRCUS OF BILLBOARDS, SIGNS, VIDEOS, IMAGES, SOUNDS AND NOISE THAT ARE ALMOST MIND-BOG-

## INTRODUCTION The Magic of Light

GLING IN THEIR PHANTASMAGORICAL PROGRESSION. BUT THE SAME IS TRUE OF THE AVENUES AND STREETS, WHOSE CLUBS AND CAFÉS TAKE ON NEW LIFE IN THE EVENING, LIKE THE IRRE-PRESSIBLE AUTOMOBILES AND YELLOW TAXICABS, WHOSE HEADLIGHTS MARK THE WAY TO THE CITY'S NIGHTLIFE. THEN THERE ARE THE STREET LIGHTS AND LANTERNS (WHICH ARE NOW ARTIFICIAL) IN CENTRAL PARK, AND THOSE IN THE SMALL HOUSES ALONG THE TREE-LINED STREETS, WHICH, IN THE MORE ISOLATED ZONES – CERTAIN STRETCHES OF THE UPPER WEST SIDE AND UPPER EAST SIDE, AND ALONG PERRY STREET AND GREENWICH STREET IN THE WEST VILLAGE, IN GRAMERCY PARK, OR EVEN IN SOME ALLEYWAYS OF HELL'S KITCHEN, ESPE-CIALLY WHEN A HORSE AND BUGGY PASS BY IN THE MIDDLE OF NIGHT – ALL REMIND US OF THE PAST OR SEEM TO ALLUDE TO A FABULOUS, TIMELESS WORLD THAT LIVES ON AND FOR THE PRESENT MOMENT.

410 • Dawn, when the sky turns pink above the Hudson River around the old pylons and the old railway on the Upper West Side.

411 • The sun rises setting the sky on fire between the high buildings of Uptown.

● Morning mist in the first rays of sun light against the skyline of New York skyscrapers, enveloping everything in a magical atmosphere.

*414-415* • The Statue
of Liberty is silhouetted
against the intense
orange and yellow early
morning sky.

*416-417* • Sometimes,
above all in winter, the
sky lights up with very
intense colors at dawn.

**418** • New York skyscrapers on a cloudy day take on almost unreal shapes and colors that contrast with the dense grayness of the sky lit by the dim light of the early morning sun.

*418-419* • The Empire State Building behind Brooklyn Bridge on a morning with truly unusual colors.

A view of Brooklyn with the sun appearing on the horizon between the silhouettes of the Manhattan skyscrapers.

422 • The skyline of the Financial District early in the morning when the sun rises on the horizon, creating a wonderful effect of contrast and light.

423 • Very early in the morning, the buildings of the Financial District are reflected in the waters of the river, creating a spectacular effect.

The skyscrapers of the Financial District, with the United Nations Plaza on the left, are illuminated by the bright early morning sunlight.

● Sometimes Brooklyn Bridge takes on the bright orange color of the sunset.

● The top of the Empire State Building is engulfed in the magic of fusing colors a little before sunset. The top of the building often changes color, to match the time of day or a certain period of the year.

As soon as darkness falls, New York is illuminated with thousands of lights that are best seen from above.

*432-433* • The port of New York, glittering with lights, with its Pier and the historic ships anchored, is particularly beautiful in the evening. The outline of the Empire State Building can be seen in the background.

*434-435* • The skyline of the city that never sleeps reflected in the calm waters of the Hudson River.

*436* • A futuristic picture of the new New York, in all its bright and intense splendor.

*436-437* • When the skyscrapers take on the colors of the night, they create an incredible contrast of shapes and colors thanks to their ultra-modern glass and steel walls.

• When it rains the lights in Times Square are reflected in the wet surface of the tarmac creating a surreal interplay of colors.

440-441 ● At night the Theater District of Broadway is illuminated with thousands of lights and colors.

442-443 ● Cars and taxis come to a standstill in the traffic among the many lights and illuminated signs of Times Square.

The lights of the
kiosk vendors merge
with those of Radio City
and the City.

446-447 • The Pier and port of New York under Brooklyn Bridge with skyscrapers in the background.

447 • The Jacob Wrey Mould Fountain was originally installed in the City Hall Park in Lower Manhattan in 1871, it was then moved to the Bronx for some time and returned here in 2000.

448 • Verrazzano-Narrows Bridge connects the districts of Staten Island and Brooklyn. It takes its name from the French explorer of Italian origin Giovanni da Verrazzano, who was the first navigator to enter the Port of New York and the Hudson River.

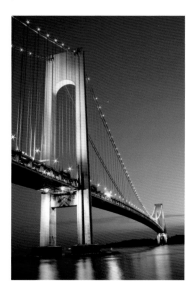

449 • The Chrysler Building with its magnificent spire, towers over the other buildings of the City. When it is illuminated it can be seen from all the major roads of Midtown.

450 • Two beams of light shooting into the sky are a glowing memorial to the Twin Towers, in this art installation entitled "Tribute in Light."

451 • The One World Trade Center Tower, better known as the Freedom Tower, is the central skyscraper of the New World Trade Center.

452-453 ● Even the various bridges that connect Manhattan with the mainland develop special light effects at night, being totally flood lit.

453 ● A view from above Midtown East at night, immediately after sunset showing the East River in the middle.

454-455 •
Cars speed towards
Brooklyn Bridge and in
the evening they create
a continuous ribbon
of lights.

456-457 •
The Manhattan skyline
is seen here from
Brooklyn, and the city
lights are reflected in
the water where they
form magnificent
rainbow.

Brooklyn Bridge is illuminated over the intense blue of the river immediately after sunset.

460 • Independence Day Fireworks in New York on 4th July.

460-461 • A view of New York and the skyline dominated by the fireworks display over the Hudson River.

# CHRISTMAS in NEW YORK

- The Rockefeller Center decorated for Christmas with the famous Christmas tree in the background, behind the ice rink.

## INTRODUCTION Christmas in New York

New York is the city of dreams. And Christmas is the time when dreams can become reality, since Santa Claus listens to children's requests for presents in the shopping centers and also talks with passers-by on the streets. The streets are decked out and glow with millions of lights. The shop windows on 5th Avenue vie with one another with their theme tableaux, and passers-by are welcomed by the Christmas trees – decorated with colored baubles, lights, tinsel, and presents lying underneath – in the gardens of the small houses and the interiors of the buildings, hotels and shopping centers. The city is in a frenzy. The museums are open. Panettone and cake are served at the art gallery openings. The restaurants and nightclubs are decorated with tinsel and organize Christmas and New Year parties, while concerts

## INTRODUCTION Christmas in New York

AND CHRISTMAS CAROLS DOMINATE THE SCENE EVERYWHERE, ALONG WITH SPECTACULAR FIREWORKS DISPLAYS THAT RING IN THE NEW YEAR. THE BIG APPLE IS IMBUED WITH A FESTIVE CHRISTMAS SPIRIT, AND NEW YORKERS ARE PARTICULARLY ELATED, CELEBRATING WITH OFFICE PARTIES AND FESTIVE GATHERINGS AT HOME OR IN THE BARS AND CAFÉS WITH FRIENDS, WHILE CHILDREN ARE AMAZED AT THE MARVELS PROPOSED BY TOY STORES SUCH AS TOYS "R" US KIDS STORE AND THE MANY ATTRACTIONS AT TIMES SQUARE, AS THE HOLIDAY SEASON IN-SPIRES THE MOST FANTASTIC CREATIONS. THERE ARE ALSO OUTDOOR CHRISTMAS MARKETS, SUCH AS THOSE IN UNION SQUARE AND BRYANT PARK, WHERE HANDICRAFTS AND SWEETS CAN BE BOUGHT AT THE MANY STALLS. AND LET US NOT FORGET THE ROMANTIC ICE RINKS, THE MOST FAMOUS OF WHICH IS ROCKEFELLER PLAZA IN ROCKEFELLER CENTER, BUILT BY JOHN D. ROCKEFELLER, WITH LUMINOUS ANGELS

# Christmas in New York

## Introduction

LEADING THE WAY TO THE TRADITIONAL CHRISTMAS TREE, WHOSE LIGHTS ARE TURNED ON EVERY YEAR IN FRONT OF A JOYFUL CROWD TO MARK THE OFFICIAL BEGINNING OF THE CHRISTMAS SEASON (TYPICALLY THE WEEK AFTER THANKSGIVING). BRYANT PARK IS THE NEW CHRISTMAS GATHERING POINT, WITH AN ICE SKATING RINK THAT ATTRACTS A LOT OF PEOPLE AND NEW YORKERS. ANOTHER ICE SKATING LOCALE IS THE CENTRAL PARK POND, IN WHICH ARE REFLECTED THE SHADOWS OF THE APARTMENT HOUSES AND HISTORIC BUILDINGS. THE POND HAS BEEN THE SETTING FOR MANY A LOVE STORY IN BOTH NOVELS AND FILMS, FOR EXAMPLE *SERENDIPITY*, STARRING JOHN CUSAK, A STORY ABOUT THE INDESCRIBABLE AND UNFORGETTABLE RANDOM OCCURRENCE OF HAPPINESS OF THE TITLE THAT IS AKIN TO MAGIC, MUCH LIKE THE CHRISTMAS SPIRIT THAT ANIMATES THE BIG APPLE.

- A house in the suburbs has been transformed into a light show, with several Christmas figures and decorations.

468-469 ● A shop in the center is covered with "Happy Holidays."

469 ● A couple take a Christmas tree home in a street in Downtown. Christmas is one of the most romantic times of the year in New York.

*470* • Just before Christmas a crowd of Father Christmases invades the city in a happy parade.

*470-471* • The Father Christmases greet the crowd as soon as they reach Times Square.

*472-473* • A heavy snowfall on 6th Avenue, near the Radio City Music Hall.

474-475 ● The gilded bronze statue of Prometheus, the symbol of the Rockefeller Center dominates the ice skating rink in winter.

475 ● An enormous Christmas tree is erected behind the statue of Prometheus and every year it is lit during a big party with music, Christmas carols and a concert attended by various celebrities including the Mayor.

Christmas decorations and water fountains embellish the center of Midtown, near the Rockefeller Center.

478-479 ● A metal toy soldier next to the Christmas lights at the Rockefeller Center.

479 ● Macy's at Christmas glittering with lights and colors, is often open 24 hours a day, so that you can even go shopping in the middle of the night.

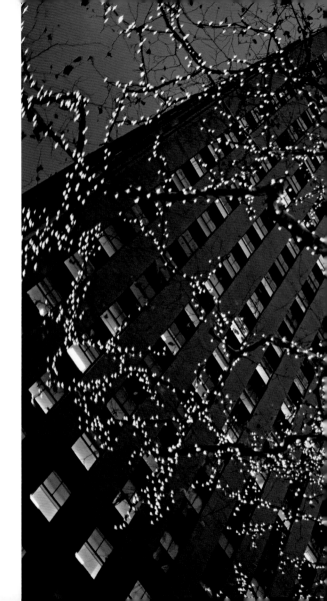

● The lights on the trees at the Rockefeller Center with skyscrapers in the background.

*482-483* • The palm tree Winter Garden at the World Financial Center in Lower Manhattan, is illuminated for Christmas.

*483* • The interior and the palm trees of the Trump Tower on 5th Avenue, are decorated for Christmas.

484-485 ● A light installation as a Christmas lighting decoration in the Financial Center.

485 ● At night the lights are lit creating an even more magical atmosphere, coloring the city with multi-colored hues.

Sacks is a favorite place for Christmas shopping and it is also famous for its beautiful window displays.

*488-489 and 489* ● Many Christmas decorations, like the ones shown in the picture at the Cartier shop, are installed on the walls of the buildings or the department stores.

*490-491* ● The Time Warner Building overlooks Central Park. It is one of the most beautiful shopping malls with several boutiques and shops. The Christmas decorations here are breathtaking.

This Christmas tree is erected next to the skyscrapers of the Bloomberg Building complex, where the Bloomberg headquarters and the financial media network are located.

494-495 • Christmas decorations in a residential neighborhood of Brooklyn. Americans love to decorate parks, gardens and house entrances with lights and illuminated figures.

496-497 • This house is in the Dyker Heights neighborhood, in Brooklyn, that has always been famous for its unique and varied Christmas decorations. New York is a melting pot of traditions and customs from the whole world even at Christmas, especially in a multi-ethnic district like Brooklyn.

**Valeria Manferto De Fabianis** is the editor of the series.
She was born in Vercelli, Italy and studied arts at the Università Cattolica del Sacro Cuore in Milan, graduating with a degree in philosophy. She is an enthusiastic traveler and nature lover. She has collaborated on the production of television documentaries and articles for the most prestigious Italian specialty magazines and has also written many photography books. She co-founded Edizioni White Star in 1984 with Marcello Bertinetti and is the editorial director.

# INDEX

# INDEX

**Alessandra Mattanza** was born with a passion for writing. She wrote her first story at the age of sixteen and dreamed of living in New York since she was a child when she was fascinated by films such as: "Sunday in New York," "Breakfast at Tiffany's," "Barefoot in the Park" and "A Witch in Paradise." This dream became reality when she decided to give up everything to go and live in New York, in pursuit of those life stories that bind the fate of all mankind, of which the Big Apple is a mirror. As a writer, journalist and photographer, she feels multi-faceted like the City that she loves and adores from its most insignificant sidewalk to the top of its stunning skyscrapers. She now feels like a true New Yorker, having lived in various neighborhoods: from Tribeca to West Village, from Murray Hill to Midtown, from Upper East Side to Upper West Side and East Village. She writes for the main Italian and German magazines and works with major publishers such as: Mondadori, Conde Nast, Rizzoli, Gruner + Jahr, Stern, Sperling & Kupfer, White Star and Giunti. She is also the author of a fictional work "Storie di New York," FBE Edizioni (2010), a collection of short stories, for which she is now producing a screenplay.

# PHOTO CREDITS

# PHOTO CREDITS

**Edward Le Poulin/Corbis:** pages 300-301, 301
**Jean-Pierre Lescourre/Agefotostock:** pages 160-161
**Richard Levine/Agefotostock:** pages 138-139
**James Leynse/Corbis:** pages 106-107
**Andrew Lichtenstein/Corbis:** pages 382-383
**Alfredo Maiquez/Agefotostock:** page 272
**Alessandra Mattanza:** pages 54, 54-55, 56-57, 60, 61, 62, 63, 64-65, 65, 78-79, 79, 101, 105, 111, 147, 182, 182-183, 235, 238, 238-239, 240-241, 242, 242-243, 244-245, 245, 246, 246-247, 258-259, 328, 328-329, 333, 374
**Patti McConville/Getty Images:** pages 98, 219, 348
**Giovanni Mereghetti/Agefotostock/Marka:** page 133
**Metzen/Getty Images:** page 483
**Michael Nagle/Getty Images:** pages 386-387, 396-397
**Netcells Limited/Getty Image:** pages 24-25
**Marvin E. Newman/Getty Images:** pages 354-355
**Robert Nickelsberg/Getty Images:** pages 358-359
**Graeme Norways/Getty Images:** pages 96-97
**Nycretoucher/Getty Images:** pages 14-15
**Eileen O'Donnell/Getty Images:** page 411
**Eva Parey/Agefotostock/Marka:** pages 278-279
**Andria Patino/Agefotostock:** pages 22-23, 434-435
**Stuart Pearce/Agefotostock:** pages 137, 139
**Stuart Pearce/Agefotostock/Marka:** pages 86-87, 276-277
**Douglas Pearson/Getty Images:** page 463
**Janette Pellegrini/Getty Images:** page 401
**Photolibrary/Agefotostock:** pages 398-399
**Ben Pipe/Travel Library/Photoshot:** page 99
**Spencer Platt/Getty Images:** pages 120-121, 234-235, 400
**Louie Psihoyos/Science Faction/Corbis:** page 220
**Radius Images/Agefotostock/Marka:** pages 349, 472-473, 478-479, 484-485
**Paul Raftery/VIEW/Corbis:** pages 222-223, 223

**Jose Fuste Raga/Agefotostock/Marka:** page 72
**Philippe Renault/Getty Images:** pages 344-345
**Ross Pictures/Corbis:** page 193
**Guido Alberto Rossi/Tips Images:** page 146
**Alan Schein Photography/Corbis:** pages 426-427
**Pietro Scozzari/Tips Images:** page 357
**Rahav Segev/Retna Ltd./Corbis:** page 163
**Jon Shireman/Getty Images:** pages 322-323
**Bryan Smith/ZUMAPRESS.com/Corbis:** pages 296-297, 383
**Johnny Stockshooter/Image State:** pages 58-59
**Rudy Sulgan/Corbis:** pages 90-91, 424-425, 467, 496-497
**SuperStock/Agefotostock/Marka:** pages 261, 340
**Ramin Talaie/Corbis:** pages 216-217, 272-273, 378
**Mario Tama/Getty Images:** pages 226, 227, 274-275
**Ray Tamarra/Getty Images:** page 305
**Murat Taner/Getty Images:** page 48
**Tetra Images/Tips Images:** page 469
**Tetra Images/Getty Images:** pages 140-141, 347
**Travelpix Ltd/Getty Image:** pages 12-13, 102-103
**Vieri Tomaselli/Agefotostock:** pages 76-77
**Julian Ungano/Getty Images:** page 120
**Lucas Vallecillos/Agefotostock:** pages 132, 422
**Rob Verhoeven & Alessandra Magni/Getty Images:** page 94
**Rudi Von Briel/Getty Images:** pages 156-157
**Ron Watts/Agefotostock/Marka:** page 39
**Craig Warga/Getty Images:** pages 270, 270-271
**Andy Welsh /Getty Images:** pages 312-313
**Nathan Willock/Agefotostock:** pages 212-213
**Barry Winiker/Getty Images:** pages 356, 485
**Corey Wise/LPI/Getty Images:** page 376
**Michael Wong/Getty Images:** pages 288-289
**Granger Wootz/Blend Images LLC/Corbis:** page 254
**Gu Xinrong/Xinhua Press/Corbis:** page 296
**Michael Yamashita/Getty Images:** pages 108-109, 237

**Michael Yamashita/National Geographic Image Collection:** page 34
**Bo Zaunders/Corbis:** pages 80-81, 200-201, 249, 292-293, 334-335
**Walter Zerla/Tips Images:** pages 134-135
**Courtesy of the MAD Museum** pages 232, 233

**Cover, from left**

**first rank:** A romantic bridge in Central Park; the Statue of Prometheus at the Rockefeller Center; Times Square. *Mitchell Funk/Getty Images, Antonio Attini/Archivio White Star, Mitchell Funk/Getty Images*

**second rank:** Empire State Building; the Statue of Liberty: detail of the entrance of the Solomon R. Guggenheim. *Antonio Attini/Archivio White Star, Michael Yamashita/Getty Images, Grant Faint/Getty Images*

**third rank:** North Cove, Lower Manhattan; Chrysler Building; aerial view of Manhattan. *Antonio Attini/Archivio White Star, Antonio Attini/Archivio White Star, Antonio Attini/Archivio White Star*

**Back cover, from left**

**first rank:** Midtown Center; some buildings in the Financial District; Bronx Botanical Gardens' Conservatory Range. *Mitchell Funk/Getty Images, 123RF, Antonio Attini/Archivio White Star*

**second rank:** General Electric Building; Central Park in winter; Westin Hotel. *Bo Zaunders/Corbis, Mitchell Funk/Getty Images, Alessandra Mattanza*

**third rank:** San Remo residential complex; Liberty Island; Trump Building. *Antonio Attini/Archivio White Star, Antonio Attini/Archivio White Star, Antonio Attini/Archivio White Star*

WHITE STAR PUBLISHERS

WS White Star Publishers® is a registered trademark
property of Edizioni White Star s.r.l.

© 2012 Edizioni White Star s.r.l.
Via M. Germano, 10
13100 Vercelli, Italy
www.whitestar.it

Translation text: Richard Pierce
Translation captions: Catherine Howard
Editing: Karen O'Brien

Cubebook® and WS Edizioni White Star® are registered trademarks property
of Edizioni White Star s.r.l.

ISBN 978-88-544-0665-0
1 2 3 4 5 6   16 15 14 13 12

Printed in China